Designed in MINNESOTA

An Exquisite Collection of
Minnesota's Finest Designers

Publishing & Design Inc.
McKinney, Texas

Published by

Publishing & Design Inc.

6900 Edge Water Drive
McKinney, Texas 75070
972-747-7866
FAX 972-747-0226
www.dsapubs.com

Publisher: Duff Tussing

Author: Anne Dullaghan

Design: Donnie Jones, The Press Group, Plano, TX

Printed in the US

PUBLISHER'S DATA

Designed in Minnesota

Library of Congress Control Number: 2007926483

ISBN Number: 0-9774451-6-X

First Printing 2007

10 9 8 7 6 5 4 3 2 1

Front Cover: Billy Beson, Bruce Kading & Renée LeJeune Hallberg,
Beson Kading Interior Design Group
See page 17

Back Cover: Betty Duff, *Design Innovations*
See page 39

Previous Page: *Macy's Interior Design Studios*
See page 105

This Page: Mark Suess, *Mark Suess Designs*
See page 139

Front Flap: Richard D'Amico, *D'Amico & Partners*
See page 33

Back Flap: Linda Engler, *Engler Skogmo Interior Design*
See page 49

Designed in MINNESOTA

An Exquisite Collection of Minnesota's Finest Designers

Author Anne Dullaghan

Introduction

Interior design is all around us. It has the power to delight, inspire, support, transform and heal. This book represents the wide variety of Minnesota's interior design talent—from bold and sophisticated to classic traditional, to understated elegance, and everything else in between. The designers whose work is shown here represent a profession dedicated to enhancing people's lives through form and function, style and substance.

Those featured in this book represent the more than fifty professional and allied interior design members of the Minnesota Chapter of the American Society of Interior Designers (ASID). ASID is the largest professional association of interior designers in the U.S. and Canada. It is a community of designers, industry representatives, educators and students committed to interior design. Through education, knowledge sharing, advocacy, community building and outreach, ASID works to advance the interior design profession and, in the process, to demonstrate and celebrate the power of design to positively change people's lives.

As you page through each designer's lavishly illustrated profile, we hope you'll gather any number of ideas from photos that feature our ASID members' concepts and creativity. From custom furniture, luxurious textiles, inventive wall treatments, and exceptional art and accessories, there's something for everyone. While our designers' projects range from to suburban homes and vacation retreats, to inventive restaurants, their work shows that truly good interior design represents fine craftsmanship and innovative ideas that accommodate a variety of design needs.

Ask any designer and they'll tell you that no matter how beautiful a room is, the only thing that matters is how the design reflects your personality and tastes. May this book inspire you to create the home of your dreams.

Anne Dullaghan

Anne Dullaghan

The Designers

Brandie Adams,
ASID, CID

Fusion Design Studio

FUSION DESIGN STUDIO

4143 Minnehaha Avenue

Minneapolis, MN 55406

612-751-6592

www.brandieadams.com

LEFT Media residence, 2005.

ABOVE RIGHT Nami Restaurant, Minneapolis 2001.

ABOVE FAR RIGHT Wayzata residence, 2006.

During her 10 years in the industry, designer Brandie Adams has been passionately designing interior spaces with meaningful, creative expressions that uniquely reflect her individual clients. Brandie uses her detail-oriented and refreshingly edgy style to work on a variety of projects in corporate design and planning, restaurant design, and residential design through her interior design firm, Fusion Design Studio.

Fusion Design Studio was born from the concept of fusing art, design, and function for all interior environments. Her studio is a small, eclectic art gallery surrounded by inspirations from local artists. Through her studio, Brandie provides full-scope interior design services for both new construction and renovation. She extends her design services to include stage and set design for the real estate market and custom art pieces she creates herself. "My passion for design reflects on my strong, repeat client relationships, my creative influence and implementation of what was once abstract and random ideas. When I work with my clients, I fuse the client's individual style with my creative edge," she says. And her clients see—and appreciate—that passion. One client remarked, "Brandie made the inherently difficult and time-consuming process of designing our home's interior as orderly, structured, and enjoyable as imaginable. Among her many great qualities as a designer, she understands the concept of working within budget and is very flexible in her style concepts. She never lets her own preferences supersede those of the client, keeps the process moving, is a lot of fun, and most important, the end result is beautiful."

Brandie has also contributed to the interior design industry through leadership and as an educator. She served seven years on the IIDA Northland Chapter Board and was president in 2001. She passed the NCIDQ exam which tests the health, safety, and welfare for the general public. Brandie has been recognized for her work including the restaurant Nami, which won "Best Design & Aesthetics, Interior Retail" from the MSCA's Retail Awards in 2001. ■

Thanks for your business! Danae

Danae Blanck Anderson, ASID, CID

I.D. Your World

I.D. YOUR WORLD

Nisswa, MN

218-330-2338 cell

218-963-0312 office/fax

idyourworld@go.com

LEFT Steve and Nancy Walsh's northwoods retreat features an artistic fireplace, created by Danae's husband, and stone mason, Jarrett, forming a focal point for their inviting greatroom.

ABOVE Capturing a cozy feel with rich color tones and hickory furniture, this time-share unit at Breezy Point Resort would make the perfect get-away spot.

ABOVE RIGHT This spacious kitchen accents the architectural details of the space with a combination of neutral tones and textures perfect for Gayle and Richard Severson's lakehome.

Other Credits: Aubrey's Interiors, Great Furniture Gallery, The Hearth Room, The Floor to Ceiling Store, Johnson's Personality Plus Interiors, Patnode Custom Cabinets, The Light Depot, Rustic Retreat Furniture, Breezy Point Resort and Carolyn Blanck

Danae Blanck Anderson was exposed to open-minded ways of thinking and expressed her creativity early in life, which has helped her throughout her career. As a young girl, she often traveled with family or friends touring historic places, capitol buildings, art galleries, and dignitaries' homes, which inspired her passion for design and art history. After graduating with a degree in interior design and mass communications/public relations from Minnesota State University, Mankato, passing the NCIDQ, becoming a CID, and working for other firms, this passion turned into her own business, I.D. Your World. Danae completes projects in both residential and commercial design—" I love the challenges and variety both types of design work have to offer," she says—and strives to capture her clients' style and personality.

Danae considers function while working with clients. "Not only should a space be beautiful, but it should also be very functional," she asserts. "Interior design affects people in so many ways, from color psychology, to slip-resistant tile in a shower or the slope of a walkway. It can be subtle or present the 'awe' factor." To then personalize her designs, Danae asks her clients many questions, and, based on their responses, does drawings, space planning, project management, color consultations, research on codes, flooring, furniture or fabric, and window coverings.

The textile designer Jack Lenor Larsen once said, "Design is everything and everything is design," and Danae agrees. "Someone had to select the light fixture above your table in the restaurant for ambience, or specify what tile pattern went where in the lobby of a hotel," she comments. "Everywhere you look, there is design. And I enjoy creating spaces that identify who my clients really are."

Holly Bayer
Allied Member ASID

Hauthaus, Inc.

HAUTHAUS, INC.

14809 Crestview Lane

Minnetonka, MN 55345

612-743-7731

holly@hauthaus.com

LEFT Timberview Trail

ABOVE RIGHT Lakeshore Circle

It was winter of 2000. Holly Bayer was stuck in a large law firm working in tech-support, far from her creative roots, and evidently struggling through the beginning of an early mid-life crisis. Right then and there, Bayer made a decision: She was going to be an interior designer.

Six years later, Bayer owns her own design company, Hauthaus, Inc., and has enjoyed no fewer than eight awards from the ASID and the National Association of the Remodeling Industry, among others. Each design is a reflection of her client's preferences, elicited throughout every step in the process, she says. She's just acting as the mirror. "Every client is incredibly unique, and my job is to help them realize his or her own style," she says. "I don't pay attention to fads, or press clients into a predestined, factory-made style, like traditional, transitional or modern. We come up with a concept together and the concept directs our selections."

Bayer, who holds a bachelor's degree in art history from Gustavus Adolphus College (cum laude) and an associate's degree from The Art Institutes International in Minneapolis, tries different things to keep her ideas fresh. She makes it a point each day to draw inspiration from something new, an artist or period, a new piece of music, or something her kids pointed out, like a pattern in the trees.

Her favorite project? Anything "brave"—or, which requires daring and confidence to produce something amazing. Take the swirling, inspired, art-nouveau kitchen which she and mentor Bonnie Birnbaum modeled on Antonio Gaudi's Casa Batllo in Barcelona.

"That is brave," she says. That is Holly. ∎

Violet Benshoof
Allied Member ASID

Josephine's Interiors, Inc.

LEFT The luxurious yet inviting great room captures the warmth of pale yellow walls and Victorian reds, enhancing a spectacular view of the Mississippi River.

ABOVE RIGHT The elegant formal dining room features beautiful Australian gum floors and an imported rug, adding the right touch of sophistication and flow into the great room.

ASID Allied Member Violet Benshoof serves her clients from one of the highest regarded studios in the St. Paul region at her full-service interior design firm, Josephine's Interiors. Josephine's Interiors boasts an extensive selection of some of the finest residential and commercial fabrics available today. One key characteristic that sets the design firm apart from its competition is an in-house workroom. The workroom also features choice reupholstery and custom furniture, all at an exceptionally competitive price. Violet was chosen to work on the restoration of the Minnesota Supreme Court partly because of the economical pricing and the expertise she brought to the project. As a preferred state vendor, Violet was selected to design the executive offices at the Minnesota State Capitol, as well as other government offices including the Office of the Attorney General, the Office of the Governor, and the Minnesota House of Representatives.

Governmental organizations gravitate toward Violet because she meets deadlines and provides quality products. Her other clients prefer to work with her over alternate designers because her style is very versatile, ranging from traditional to contemporary, and because she keeps them in mind rather than taking over with a formula. From the smallest of projects to a complete redesign—her specialty is renovation and intricately detailed restoration—Violet is particularly apt at reflecting her clients' personalities and lifestyles in all of her design work with an extra touch for less cost. All in all, you could say that she reflects the Josephine's Interiors' motto, "From floors to walls, we do it all."

For commercial projects, Violet offers color, textile, and furnishing consultation services, as well as space plans for a small fee. As Josephine's Interiors' principal designer and owner, Violet can easily provide window treatments that aid in sun control without detracting from exterior views, resilient flooring materials including government-approved and scheduled eco-polymeric flooring for high-traffic endurance. Josephine's Interiors is only one of a select few dealers that can offer this flooring. For residential projects, Violet enjoys working closely with her clients to coordinate fabrics and textures in a manner that pleases the most discerning customer in bedroom ensembles, living room environments, and window covering. Violet's philosophy on design is summed up in the doctrine, "You may not know what you want, but you certainly know what you do not like." She ambitiously takes on the venture of uncovering what her clients are looking for in design like she did for one of her favorite restoration projects, the Armstrong-Quinlan House in St. Paul. When new owners took on

ABOVE LEFT This area includes state-of-the-art appliances and warm cherry cabinetry, designed for the gourmet cook to be able to interact with guests.

LEFT The picture framed arched window enhances the view of the Mississippi River and downtown area for a relaxing atmosphere in the master bedroom.

the hefty task of restoring the historic property—a house built in 1886 that uniquely blends different architectural styles—into four elegant new condominiums, Violet received the exciting opportunity to work on every aspect of design for the restoration including the flooring, interiors, exterior lighting, kitchens, bathrooms, color selections, furnishings, and accessories.

When Violet is not tending to a wide realm of design projects she is gourmet cooking, collecting dolls, enjoying music, or dancing; activities that reflect her artistry as much as her designs do. ▪

JOSEPHINE'S INTERIORS, INC.

1440 Arcade Street

St. Paul, MN 55106

651-776-2731

www.josephinesinteriors.com

RIGHT The original restored staircase greets guests and draws the eye upward to the magnificent pewter chandelier. Note the whimsical umbrella stand under the stairwell.

BELOW The mosaic surround of the temperature controlled Jacuzzi and coordinated walk-in shower area, reflected in the vanity mirror, is the perfect place to unwind.

Billy Beson, ASID, CID, Bruce Kading, ASID, CID & Renée LeJeune Hallberg, Allied Member ASID

Beson Kading Interior Design Group

LEFT Beson defines the new age "rec room." This vibrant multifunctional space is an underground oasis. Beson used a warm sunny color palette with colorful accents to complement this contemporary estate on beautiful Lake Minnetonka.

BELOW You choose—shoot pool, enjoy a cocktail or lounge in the scrumptious theatre.

Billy Beson, ASID, CEO of Beson Kading Interior Design Group has developed an elite high-end clientele with projects spanning from a private island in Hawaii to Vail, Chicago, Palm Beach, and most importantly, at home in Minnesota. Beson is best known for the diversity of his work. His style ranges from ultra modern to the very most traditional and everything in between. Each and every project is an expression of the client's personality, specific needs, and individuality. "The best part of my design is that no two projects look alike," says Beson. Having extremely different projects keeps Billy on his toes and always eager to learn new things.

Bruce Kading, ASID, President of Beson Kading Interior Design Group brings over thirty years of experience to this talented group of design professionals. "Our staff consisting of four interior designers and a support staff of 10 is the ideal size to enable us to offer impeccable design service supported by top notch customer service" says Kading. Open communication and an honest exchange of ideas is a hallmark of his design philosophy. The results are beautiful, functional, and original environments and a delighted, loyal clientele. Bruce's style reflects a collected look that appears to have evolved over time with ease. His impeccable sense of detail is evident throughout every project from the finest of architectural details to the perfect pillow. "I like to mix dressy with casual, blending textures, patterns, and colors to create the perfect balance within a space."

LEFT The asymmetrical grouping of old world oil paintings create the perfect background for a rare collection of objet d'art.

FACING PAGE A sense of history and old world charm is created by blending antiques with reproductions from many periods and styles.

Beson Kading's Renée LeJeune Hallberg is the perfect complement to the interior design team. Her flair for creating classic and understated design adds an air of timeless beauty and contemporary style to her environments. She often combines antiques and new furnishings to invent comfortable interiors with rich layers of color, texture, and warmth. "I create spaces that my clients' cannot wait to come home to," says LeJeune Hallberg. "I love designing spaces where life is celebrated with family and friends." LeJuene

ABOVE This room celebrates family and the art of fine dining. A collection of oil paintings add color and richness to the refined and elegant space.

Hallberg's experience plays a prominent role in all aspects of her design from space planning, lighting design, and furniture layout, to selecting the perfect accessories to complete her environments.

A key element of the mission of Beson Kading Interior Design Group is taking their passion and talents into their community to empower those in need. The design group is involved with the Minnesota Orchestra, The Greater Minneapolis Crisis Nursery and Smile Network International just to name a few. "Our community has been so gracious to all of us it seems natural that we give back" says Beson.

BESON KADING INTERIOR DESIGN GROUP

275 Market Street, Suite 530

Minneapolis, MN 55405

612-338-8187 F: 612-338-2462

www.besonkading.com

Jaque Bethke,
Allied Member ASID
COI Design

LEFT Honed limestone flooring and hand-waxed walls in the kitchen provide a backdrop for the open kitchen and dining area. Glass pendants hang in circles of light over the glass snack bar and granite countertops where guests can gather.

ABOVE RIGHT Sumptuous granite sculpts the floors and walls of this master bathroom. The countertops are four inches thick and are topped by frosted glass mirrors and windows allowing natural light into the space while keeping your privacy.

Jaque Bethke inherited her sense of creativity from her mother, a professional knitter and music lover, and her father, a professional car designer for racecar drivers, entertainers, and antique collectors. Then she built upon these talents while working in Las Vegas in the fields of architecture, engineering, and design, where she learned to incorporate the elements of surprise and grandeur. Today, Jaque excels in residential architecture and interiors, commercial design, lighting design, cabinet design, landscape design, and urban planning, but she believes that her greatest gift is the ability to read people and their situations because she can use it to determine the direction in which her clients want to go.

Jaque is committed to retaining the integrity of the design in all of her projects and is particularly proud when she is able to do it for complex projects. A student of Frank Lloyd Wright design and a follower of Neutra and Mies van der Rohe, when assessing projects, Jaque tries to imagine what they might have done with each site, the client, and the materials. "Their ability to create just the right balance of clean lines coupled with a material palette of warmth made their work perfection," she explains. "I am passionate about design and excited by good design."

While she may be hard on herself, Jaque understands what constitutes success. She is now celebrating her second year in a newly constructed studio with her practice COI Design. Spacious at 5,500 square feet and fully capable with four employees, Jaque's studio integrates all of the architectural components necessary to complete a project and the knowledge to execute the details. Such details are extremely important to her because they

are what make a great project, she insists. "In my experience, most problematic projects do not go wrong because of the big picture," she remarks. "They go wrong because nobody paid attention to the details."

Jaque has been published in *Midwest Home and Garden*, *Home Builder*, *Luxury Home*, and *Mpls.St.Paul Magazine*, and she has been honored over the years with numerous industry awards. Her awards, no doubt, are a result of her thoroughness and the pursuit of excellence that has consistently driven her throughout her 19-year career. If Jaque is designing a night club, she wants it to be the most successful club around, not only in terms of aesthetics, but also in terms of sales. And, again, the quality of design is paramount, whether she is designing interiors

ABOVE Like the exterior, the interior architecture takes its cues from classic elements, as exemplified by the barrel vault, drawing your eyes from the front to the back. Limestone, wool carpet, and hand rubbed walls set the tone as you enter, while the furnishings offer natural textures and the original artwork offers color.

for residential or commercial clients. "If you put the wrong knob on the door, no matter how wonderful the veneer, the overall look is compromised," she says. "Miss one thing and you end up with mediocrity or worse."

For Jaque, design is her life. She sees room for improvement everywhere she goes, looking beyond the initial impression to the deeper details. With this propensity, it is no wonder why so many choose Jaque as their designer. ■

COI DESIGN

1362 Hamel Road

Medina, MN 55340

763-478-3946

jaque@coidesign.net

www.coidesign.net

An eye catching railing, stainless steel accents, glass tile floors, and maple form the building blocks of the lower level bar and adjoining entertainment area. With its innovative art, architecture, and design, this room exudes style.

The dining room walls provide a backdrop for the floating console and fireplace. The furniture repeats the circular shapes and mixed wood composition while an oil painting by Bauman provides a pop of color.

Bonnie Birnbaum, ASID, CID

Bonnie Birnbaum Interiors

BONNIE BIRNBAUM INTERIORS

190 Interlachen Lane

Excelsior, MN 55331

612-803-8120

bonniebirnbaum@msn.com

Founded on an education in nursing from John Hopkins University, art history from Hunter College, and interior design from Parsons School of Design, Bonnie Birnhaum takes a more personal approach to interior design than most others in her field. "I put together the nurturing and people skills of nursing with the artistic aspects of art history, and decided to go to school for interior design," she says. As a result, Bonnie approaches projects with an "It's all about you" mentality, taking clients' ideas and translating them into colorful and creative designs that reflect their desires.

Bonnie first conducts extensive interviews with clients, and then develops a concept with the philosophy, "Begin with the end in mind." Inspired by extensive travel to historic architectural sites, Bonnie is able to complete projects such as a kitchen remodel she did in a historic home, where she created a helical vault inspired by an interior designed by the architect Gaudi. And her work certainly does not go unnoticed. As a member of ASID and a Certified Interior Designer, Bonnie received people's choice awards in 1998, 2000, 2002, 2004, 2005, and 2006, from *Mpls. St. Paul Magazine* as well as recognition by winning ASID Awards for projects in 2005.

Just as her designs are a reflection of her clients' desires, they are also a reflection of the balance she seeks in her own life. Outside of work, the former Minnesota ASID chapter president enjoys traveling, gardening, cooking, and spending time with her grandchildren. And what better way to bring fulfillment and balance to her clients—as she has been doing for 30 years—than to pursue fulfillment and balance for herself. ■

LEFT "Norman" interior. The stone walls and wood beams are all faux painted.

ABOVE The Antonio Gaudi inspired helical vault is the focal point in this historic house.

ABOVE RIGHT The historic boats that sailed Lake Minnetonka provide the inspiration for this porch overlooking the lake.

Georgia Cox, Allied Member ASID

Georgia's Creations, Inc.

GEORGIA'S CREATIONS, INC.

dba Interiors by Decorating Den

1842 26th Avenue NW

New Brighton, MN 55112

651-633-7854

g46georgia@comcast.net

LEFT Georgia designed this award-winning home office to provide excellent functionailty with a warm, comfortable living room feel. The palladium windows afford great natural lighting and a lake-front view and are enchanced by hand-painted trompe l'oeil scarves and a stained-glass window.

ABOVE RIGHT Georgia created this living room for a couple with differing tastes—the husband preferred contemporary while the wife loved traditional.

It did not take long for Georgia Cox to receive recognition for her design work. After establishing her Interiors by Decorating Den franchise in 1994, she received five first-place awards, as well as designation as Decorator of the Year in 2000. She has also been published in *Woman's World*, *Windows Fashions*, *Home Office Computing*, and *Draperies & Window Coverings*, and was also a featured decorator in the hardcover books *Smart and Simple Decorating* by Time-Life Books and *Creating Great Guest Rooms*. In addition, Georgia placed second in *Window Fashions Magazine's* Window Fashion Design Competition in 1998.

Throughout her life, Georgia has been drawn to, and has excelled in, the creative arts—from fashioning award—winning floral designs and cooking, to decorating her home with her own oil paintings. She is an Allied Member of ASID and a member of IFDA, currently captain on a local United States Tennis Association team. She's also served her community through a wide variety of volunteer and community organizations, including the local school board, remedial children's programs, and the American Federation of Garden Clubs. In her spare time, she enjoys traveling with her husband. First and foremost in her profession and community, though, is each of her clients. "For me, the excitement of having my own decorating business comes in meeting the many challenges of creative design, time management, organizational discipline, and customer interaction, but the true reward is in the smile of a satisfied client," she says.

Michal Crosby
Allied Member ASID

Michal Crosby Interiors, Inc.

MICHAL CROSBY INTERIORS, INC.

275 Market Street, Suite 369

Minneapolis, MN 55405

612-339-3937

design@mcinteriors.com

LEFT Striking hand-embroidered draperies, coordinating with the antique oriental rug, frame the view of the woods in this European style living room.

ABOVE Copper metal cabinet doors with frosted and carved glass add a lustrous sheen to this bath/changing room off the pool area.

ABOVE RIGHT This sunroom/family room provides a cozy, yet elegant, retreat. The coffered ceiling and hand-carved columns add stunning old-world detail to a new addition.

Undoubtedly one of Michal Crosby's favorite projects was a contemporary condominium overlooking downtown Minneapolis that she designed for a client who harkened from a traditional home in the country. By utilizing the client's traditional furnishings in the new contemporary setting, she incorporated the part of her client's personality that related to a more rural environment. This integrated approach is one she takes quite often. "I design interiors that comprehensively express my clients' personalities," she states. "If their best friend walks into their newly designed home and says, 'This is so you!,' it is the biggest compliment I could receive."

Michal Crosby Interiors was established in 1984 and specializes in unique residential design. The full-service firm works with various teams of architects, builders, tradespeople, and many artisans to implement different styles of design. As a result of this personal attention, her clients keep coming back. "We have quite a few clients who have been with us for 15 to 20 years," she says. "I think this speaks of our commitment to excellence."

To add further uniqueness to the services that Michal Crosby Interiors provides, twice a year Michal attends design shows in Paris, such as Maison et Objet, and the domestic High Point Furniture Market. When she is not working hard carrying out her clients' modes of self expression and uncovering complementary pieces to fit into their homes, she finds leisurely balance in her family, reading, running, traveling, cooking, and ballroom dance. ∎

Richard D'Amico, Allied Member ASID

D'Amico & Partners

LEFT The Lurcat bar is an eclectic mix of styles and colors with Italian chandeliers, blue Venetian plaster and faux marble finishes.

ABOVE *Bar Lurcat:* Exposed brick provide contrast to the gold Venetian plaster and café tables are mixed with furniture groupings throughout the space.

ABOVE RIGHT *Café Lurcat:* A private dining area has the feel of a European café with white cloth drum lighting, colorful murals and crisp white tablecloths.

Richard D'Amico's roots in the restaurant industry date back to 1954, when his first-generation Italian-American parents, Art and Helen, opened D'Amico Restaurant in a small roadhouse just outside of Cleveland, Ohio. In the 1980s, Richard allied with his brother to transform the modest business into a popular Continental restaurant complete with tableside cooking. And this was just the beginning for Richard and restaurant design.

Richard went on to found his management consulting business in contracts and concept development in 1982, D'Amico & Partners, and lure his brother away from the family establishment with the proposition to open their own restaurant, D'Amico Cucina. Actualizing his interest in art, architecture, and design, Richard decided to design the restaurant himself. D'Amico Cucina became a Twin Cities destination that immediately received wide acclaim, igniting a personal trend in restaurant design for many endeavors to come.

Richard does not fulfill the traditional role of CEO for his various venues these days. His passion focuses on the design and development of new restaurant concepts, which amount to 18 in Minnesota and three in Florida, and he has done so with notable success.

In 1980, he opened Azur, and with its stunning, high-design interior and robust Provencal and Basque cuisine, the restaurant wowed the Twin Cities and the nation, and solidified the D'Amicos' reputation as the region's preeminent restaurateurs. Azur received Honorable Mention in the Restaurant Hotel Design International Award competition in 1980, awards in *Designer Specifier* magazine, first place in the ASID Minnesota Chapter design competition, and the Best of Show award from the National Chapter of ASID.

ABOVE *Masa:* The pastel and white décor is punctuated by iridescent green glass tiles forming a rolling wave wall, a perfect complement to the gold-flecked walls.

In 1991, he revealed Bocce, a flamboyant sports bar with avant-garde decor, which included a stuffed giraffe and a bocce court, which received Honorable Mention in the ASID Minnesota Chapter design competition. In 1995, he developed an Italian concept, Campiello, which received an ASID Minnesota Chapter award, and in 2000, another new concept, Café and Bar Lurcat, received the Best in Real Estate Design Award from the *Minnesota Business Journal*, as well as praise for the space's Interior Renovation from the *Minneapolis/ St. Paul Business Journal*.

Most recently, Masa, the contemporary white-cloth Mexican restaurant he designed and opened, received the Fresh, Artistic, and Brilliant (FAB) Award from the Northland Chapter of the International Interior Design Association. Richard spent time in Mexico City and the Baja Peninsula soaking up the food, culture and design in preparation for his new concept and claims the greatest surprise in his 25-plus years of hospitality experience is the success of Masa. "If someone had told me 20 years ago that we would ultimately design and operate a Mexican restaurant, I would have thought they were crazy," Richard comments.

Since Richard founded D'Amico & Partners, he has led the company through a period of rapid growth, currently generating over 50 million dollars in revenue annually. For continued inspiration, he explores new ideas and trends from European design magazines and the Milan furniture fair, where he goes to find products not available in the United States. His passion for excellence and innovation in design is unwavering and even proclaimed in the company's mission statement.

"To apply the highest standards of creativity and excellence to…the creation of inviting and comfortable restaurants." ▪

D'AMICO & PARTNERS

211 North First Street, #175

Minneapolis, MN 55401

612-374-1776 F: 612-374-1869

richard@damico.com

www.damico.com

BELOW LEFT *Masa Bar:* A juicy orange backlit bar offers a welcoming setting.

BELOW *Masa:* Modern furniture was selected for its simplicity and clean lines while tile-framed notebook sketches of Mexican high fashion reinforce the theme of elegant sophistication.

Heidi Dockter, Allied Member ASID

Heidi Dockter Interior Design

HEIDI DOCKTER INTERIOR DESIGN

6617 Promontory Drive

Eden Prairie, MN 55346

952-937-9728

heididockter@comcast.net

LEFT Once stark and uninviting, Heidi Dockter added comfort and warmth to this living room with the use of walnut floors and woodworking, lighting and large-scale furniture.

ABOVE Granite countertops and glazed-painted cabinetry help make this kitchen an inviting place to be.

ABOVE RIGHT This dining room has an Old World ambiance enhanced by its faux-painted wall and mood lighting.

Heidi Dockter Interior Design offers its clients more than the trade itself. While the firm provides a complete range of services—its team reviews architectural drawings and finish specifications, as well as handles lighting, furnishings, wall finishes, window treatments, accessories, and art—perhaps its greatest strength is Heidi's ability to develop positive interactive relationships with clients. After carefully listening to clients to determine their distinct styles, personalities, and lifestyles, the Heidi Dockter Interior Design team then strengthens the relationships by embodying integrity, developing trust, and encouraging communication.

The firm's founder, Heidi Dockter, has had a passion for interior design since she was 12 years old. "I began my career in a prominent furniture/design studio in Scottsdale, Arizona," she explains. Now 22 years into her career—12 of them in the Twin Cities—she approaches all of her projects with the mission to create distinctive interiors that emanate sophistication, comfort, and warmth in timeless environments that reflect her clients' tastes and lifestyle. "I am comfortable designing contemporary, traditional, and transitional interiors," she says. "I just apply the essentials of good design and combine these with an innate sense of style." From conception to purchase to installation, Heidi seamlessly combines every detail to create unparalleled design. Supported by time-honored associations with reputable architects, custom builders, and remodelers, it is no wonder why Heidi has received recognition in *Mpls. St. Paul Magazine, Midwest Home and Garden, Phoenix Magazine, Phoenix Home & Garden,* and the *Minneapolis Star Tribune.*

Betty Duff,
Allied Member ASID
Design Innovations

Having worked with Grammy Award-winning record producers Jimmy Jam Harris and Terry Lewis, NBA MVP Kevin Garnett, NBA All-Star Chancy Billups, and late Hall of Fame baseball player Kirby Puckett, Betty Duff is definitely one of the more well-known interior designers in the Twin Cities. One of the reasons these celebrities and many other local clients come to Betty is because she often visits design centers across the country to grasp new design concepts before they hit the Twin Cities market. These excursions ensure that her clients have the greatest number of options in design as possible, from the most traditional to the most contemporary of styles. As an independent, one-person design firm, Betty also offers hands-on, personalized customer service from the stage of planning spaces to the stage of accessorizing them.

Betty first discovered that interior design was her occupational calling during high school in Tyler, Texas, when she was given the opportunity to create window displays for the popular retailer Pier One in 1969. She then decided to study interior design at the University of Texas at Austin and later established her firm in 1987. Now an ASID Allied member and IFDA member, Betty believes that function comes first and frill comes second. For each project, she interviews her clients, focuses on the positive elements of their existing design, and then partners with them to fulfill their mutually agreed upon design goals. When she started working with Jimmy James Harris and Terry Lewis, after interviewing them and understanding their needs concerning their studio, Flyte Tyme Studios in Edina, the project turned out to be one of her favorites. Betty also very much enjoyed designing a 37,000-square-foot Minnesota home, and Harmony Ranch in Westlake Village, California.

Betty further fulfills her role as a creditable designer by sustaining a relationship with her local design center, an exercise that she believes every good designer should do, particularly because it can lead to valuable referrals. "The director of International Market Square was kind enough to refer me—as one of five female independent designers—to a woman lawyer who had made senior partner at a local law firm," she remembers. "I had just founded my own firm and the project led to creating the spaces for 10 other partners' offices, all thanks to a simple phone call from the design center's director." This experience taught Betty to refrain from pre-judging situations and to always follow through, even if it just means returning a phone call —because you never know where that phone call will lead.

ABOVE Barrel-vaulted bathroom features faux painted stone elements while utilizing onyx materials for walls and floors. Faux painting by Lizeanne Geno.

FACING PAGE Steps away from the exterior pool, this area features a bamboo ceiling with colorful accents in stone, fabrics and artifacts collected from around the world.

As for her life outside of design, Betty enjoys spending time with her loving family and fabulous friends, and she finds personal contentment in her faith in the Lord. By rounding out her professional life with her personal interests, she knows how to focus on what is important to her clients and how to incorporate those priorities into her designs.

DESIGN INNOVATIONS

6133 Blake Ridge Road

Edina, MN 55346

952-903-5152

bduff1128@aol.com

Mary Dworsky, ASID, CID

Mary Dworsky Interior Design

MARY DWORSKY INTERIOR DESIGN

275 Market Street, Suite 451

Minneapolis, MN 55405

612-339-0070

mary@marydworskyid.com

LEFT A fireplace clad in stained metal and a custom storage unit in wenge was designed to coordinate with the Christian Liaigre cocktail table and sofas.

ABOVE The dining room and kitchen repeat the wenge wood and bring in stainless steel and glass for the backsplash and red accents to warm the limestone floored spaces.

ABOVE RIGHT The antique fireplace sets the ambiance for this grand North Woods retreat.

For more than 30 years Mary Dworsky of Mary Dworsky Interior Design has been creating award-winning interiors for her clients. In 2000, Mary formed her own firm, Mary Dworsky Interior Design, which is located in International Market Square's Design Center.

Mary's designs have won numerous awards including the prestigious ASID Designer of Distinction Award in 2005. She is passionate about her design and it is reflected in the interiors she creates for her clients, whether it's just one room or a whole house. Great design also needs exceptional service and Mary excels in this. She was awarded by the Governor of Minnesota the Quality Service Award from the Minnesota Council for Quality Service.

Giving back to the community is an important priority to Mary. She has given her time to help design an apartment building for homeless teens, a group home for mentally ill woman and their children, and is the current President of Quota International of Minneapolis, a nonprofit organization that raises money for disadvantaged women and children, as well as hard of hearing and deaf persons around the world. Mary also was the President of the Minnesota chapter of ASID, and has held many other board positions.

Mary listens closely to her clients and collaborates with architects, contractors and crafts people to design entire homes, kitchens, remodeling projects or aging in place projects to create inspired environments for the way her clients live. ▪

Michele Eich
Allied Member ASID

Eich Interior Design

Michele Eich was designing a model home when somebody suggested that she should make up a business card. When the model home opened a couple of weeks later, that business card led to many phone calls, giving Michele the opportunity to launch her own firm. Now 10 years later, Michele's mom runs the retail store portion of Eich Interior Design—the store features a unique and fun inventory from which Michele pulls for her clients —while Michele works out of the firm's design studio, distinguishing Eich Interior Design from its competitors as a welcoming family-run business.

Particularly inviting about the firm is Michele's very energetic personality and hands-on style. She loves to be on the jobsite and does not hesitate to pick up a power tool when needed. "I am willing to get my hands dirty, but I love to be feminine and 'designer-y' as well," she remarks. "If I was not doing this, I would be racing cars for Victoria's Secret and my car would be pink." While her racecar is only a vision, her designs are anything but. Michele adeptly materializes casual elegance for both residential and commercial projects, blending contemporary and traditional styles to create unpredictable interiors. She often mixes styles, such as Asian with traditional, to reflect the varied tastes of her clients. Preferring to break up pattern, Michele incorporates her clients' design ideas with her own and then shows them how to take the results to the next level.

Most of Michele's clients come to her after seeing a showcase home she did or another project on which she worked, but they stay because of her charismatic character and ability to earn their trust. "I take on the role of a psychologist to learn about the most intimate details of my clients' lives," she explains. "Then I encourage them to trust me to bring out their personalities in my designs, especially if they cannot visualize or articulate what they want." From there, Michele finds inspiration in the elements that ultimately make up her designs. She loves natural or man-made products that reflect beauty, such as an ornamental faucet, and colors that trigger memories and stimulate minds.

If given the opportunity to work on a chef or fashion designer's home, Michele would jump right on it. "I would really enjoy working side-by-side with somebody who has a unique job," she says. "A chef sees colors a little differently and needs function in a kitchen; I would have so much fun designing both." Michele started imagining how she would design certain interiors when she was a young girl. While sitting at her kitchen table, she often drew

ABOVE LEFT 2005 ASID Showcase Home —Master Suite Bath. Minneapolis, MN (Kenwood, Lake of the Isles).

LEFT 2003 ASID Showcase Home—Master Bedroom. Minneapolis, MN (Lake Harriet).

up house plans that included a swimming pool and dream bedrooms. When her parents did decide to redecorate their home, Michele went to a local wallpaper store and put together samples and paint colors. She has come a long way since; her work has been published in *Mpls St Paul Magazine* and *Midwest Home & Garden*, and she just finished working with "Hometime," a television program covering home improvement on PBS.

EICH INTERIOR DESIGN

3150 Spruce Street

Little Canada, MN 55117

612-325-1360 F: 612-331-1435

eichinterior@qwest.net

ABOVE RIGHT 2006 ASID Showcase Home— Kitchen. Wayzata, MN (Lake Minnetonka).

RIGHT 2005 ASID Showcase Home—Master Suite. Minneapolis, MN (Kenwood, Lake of the Isles).

BELOW 2005 ASID Showcase Home—Master Suite. Minneapolis, MN (Kenwood, Lake of the Isles).

Linda Engler, ASID
& Talla Skogmo, ASID

Engler Skogmo Interior Design

LEFT Classic, colorful and casual... the client's mandate for this family gathering space. Rich saturated colors embrace the room while the crisp white millwork adds the counterpoint.

ABOVE This former dining room breathes new life as the study with work space for two. Walnut, leather and a vibrant striped fabric combine to create a warm and productive haven ready for work or repose.

ABOVE RIGHT Colorful tranquility awaits in this idyllic wooded setting. This screen porch's simplicity is enhanced, not overpowered, by seagrass, soft down and a playful mix of color and pattern.

Big picture thinking to the smallest detail. This statement sums up the design approach of Linda Engler and Talla Skogmo, cofounders of Engler Skogmo Interior Design. In the years following their education at the University of Minnesota, Linda and Talla's paths continued to cross in Twin Cities design circles as they advanced their careers. The two came to realize that they shared very similar design and business philosophies and ultimately decided to turn serendipity into success by combining their years of experience to form Engler Skogmo Interior Design in 2003. "The enthusiastic support we received from the design community, vendors, and clients was remarkable and heart warming" says Talla of the firm's launch.

Balancing a successful business with busy family lives, Linda and Talla have grown Engler Skogmo into a team of seven professionals working out of their studio in Edina, Minnesota. With a client base primarily in the Twin Cities, this ASID award winning firm's work can also be found across the region and the country. "Our business is human" says Linda. "We develop a deep understanding of our clients that often ends in friendship." In addition to the design awards, the firm's work has appeared in local and national publications.

Engler Skogmo focuses on the entire design process—from the initial interview, space plan and construction material specification through furniture selection, art, accessories and the final installation. Linda and Talla have compiled a team of professionals that works cohesively when partnering with architects, contractors and consultants. Building long term relationships with vendors, coupled with a detailed knowledge of products, enables the firm's designers to guide the client through an efficient and thorough decision making process. This collaborative approach results in a project team driven by the big picture, all the while minding the details that will bring that picture into focus.

LEFT A massive stone hearth anchors the conversation area of this timber framed multi-generational family retreat in the north woods. A desire for a timeless and collected interior results in a fresh, original composition—a counter to staid and trite cabin décor.

BELOW This kitchen is the workhorse of the retreat. It offers high tech function in an organic shell.

Design talent alone does not guarantee success. Linda and Talla believe that their attention to the business side of owning a company differentiates the firm. "We stress professionalism in our business practices and believe it is equal to the creative aspects of our design," explains Talla. Engler Skogmo's focus on high-end custom product requires strong systems and an organized approach to keep orders on track. The energy level and atmosphere in the studio is also attractive to staff and clients and adds to the experience. "We are passionate about what we do and it shows," states Linda. "We often hear clients and vendors say that they pick up a 'good vibe' when they visit us—and they should. The whole design experience should be energizing." ■

ENGLER SKOGMO INTERIOR DESIGN

5100 Edina Industrial Blvd., Suite 200

Edina, MN 55439

952-746-2007 F: 952-746-2008

www.englerskogmo.com

ABOVE RIGHT Elegant curves punctuate the lobby of this luxury condominium development. A mix of travertine, deep wood tones, vibrant textiles and an Italian crystal chandelier creates a sophisticated and grand welcome.

RIGHT The grand welcome continues in the community room appointed with gracefully silhouetted furniture gathered around a classic stone mantelpiece.

Christine Frisk
ASID, CID
Alternative Designs

Even as a child, Christine Frisk loved manipulating space. She would spend hours arranging and rearranging her room's interior design. Today, the owner of Alternative Designs in Minneapolis, still relates strongly to the effects that spaces have on people. Her clients set the style of a project, and she brings their desires to life.

"I am not out to force a particular style on my clients," she says. "I work closely with them to create an interior that completes their thoughts and ultimately tells their story, whether it's a commercial or residential space."

In addition to holding a bachelor of science degree in interior design from the University of Minnesota, Christine is a past vice president of the Minnesota chapter of American Society of Interior Designers, a past president of the Minnesota Interior Design Legislative Action Committee, and a current ASID member.

Although Christine started out in commercial practice designing large-scale corporate, health-care and retail spaces, she now applies her professional experience to home interiors, as well as the occasional restaurant or commercial project. Because her initial projects required a great deal of technical specification, Christine has grown accustomed to designing and specifying the products attached to the structure itself. Not just lights and trim, but the flow and details of the interior as they relate to functionality: how a client works and lives in their space.

Her favorite projects allow her to work with this "built environment"—the selection of materials that are attached to the structure, including the design of the space itself as well as the cabinets and lighting. "Lighting is everything," she says. "It brings to the design to life."

Furniture, while important, becomes the accessory for the backdrop Christine loves creating. Having the opportunity to select these items along with the finishes creates a space "where all things are having the same conversation," she says.
The first step in creating a great design for a client is to find out how a space will really be used—something Frisk notes that many interior designers don't spend enough time doing. From this, she creates the initial design, which is revised with the client's input and developed in detailed drawings. When designers don't give enough time to this process, mistakes often follow. "My philosophy is to stay interested and to really be a good listener. If you are talented at design but don't listen to your client, you have missed the boat entirely."

As a space is built, Christine holds weekly meetings with everyone involved, massaging details and solving problems. Getting the parties to work together as a team is a rewarding process, she says, and only enhances the finished product. This is especially true when clients stay involved. "Projects where the clients are actively engaged are the most successful," she says. "There are few surprises, and the finished interior tells their story. I love when I can walk into a space and think to myself, this is really about the client, their life, and their experiences." ■

ABOVE LEFT Five Restaurant and Street Lounge, Minneapolis. Stairwell and Bistro.

LEFT Five Restaurant and Street Lounge, Minneapolis. Main Floor Lounge.

ALTERNATIVE DESIGNS

275 Market Street, Suite 469

Minneapolis, MN 55405

612-659-1775 F: 612-659-1725

christine@altdes.com

RIGHT Long Lake, Minnesota Residence. Kitchen.

BELOW RIGHT Minneapolis Residence. Family Room.

BELOW Long Lake, Minnesota Residence. Billiard Bar.

Gabberts Design Studio & Fine Furnishings

Randy Nelson, ASID, Jennifer Sheffert, Allied Member ASID & Nancy Woodhouse, Allied Member ASID

Gabberts Design Studio & Fine Furnishings' doors open up to a 78,000-square-foot world of design treasures, offering customers unique furnishings, accessories and accent pieces arranged in three lifestyles, further defined by a series of "viewpoints." Custom design options in upholstery, case goods, window treatments, wall and floor coverings, give customers unlimited choice, through a team of professional, award-winning designers who make it easy to create beautiful homes that are a reflection of their clients. The Gabberts Design Studio helps each customer find the designer who is best suited to their personal style allowing the design process to be easy and the interiors to be a true reflection of them.

One of these expert designers, Jennifer Sheffert, has been designing for more than 20 years, the majority of which have been with Gabberts. After working for another large firm, she joined the esteemed Gabberts team to more completely service clients with its elaborate showroom and access to all of the resources she needs, including fabrics, furnishings, floor coverings, and many one-of-a-kind accessories. As a comprehensive, "one-stop shop," she is able to provide her customers with everything they need for a beautiful home. Jennifer is enthusiastic working as a Gabberts designer not only because of the comprehensive support she receives and can therefore afford her clients, but also because Gabberts offers her resources which extend far beyond the showroom, to create a special home for her clients.

Customers seek Jennifer for her award-winning design talent to design spaces that reflect how they live. "Gabberts provides the support I need to concentrate on exceptional design," she says. "I can meet with clients, develop design based on their wants and needs, order the appropriate furnishings, and get everything delivered and installed in a timely manner." Jennifer focuses on residential projects, particularly 10,000-square-foot and up, for which she creates inviting, warm, and cozy interiors while she remains conscious of scale, texture, and lighting. Inspired by her aunt—who was an interior designer—Jennifer is now inspired by fashion, color, pattern and textural trends, travel, nature, the fine arts and architecture.

Randy Nelson is another proud Gabberts designer who loves working with the 60-year-old legacy brand known for its unique high-end furnishings and design resources. He is inspired by the entire team of designers, and enjoys working with them. "We help each other by sharing ideas and inspirations," he says. Randy's expertise is uniquely founded on his previous role as an educator. He taught interior design for

ABOVE LEFT Edina 2005 Parade Home
Jennifer Sheffert, Allied Member ASID

LEFT Whitney Landmark Residence
Karen Soojian, ASID, Sarah Bernardy, Allied Member ASID,
Karlene Hunter Baum, Allied Member ASID

several years at a community college in southern California, which motivated him to master the material and concepts of the business. He is an avid believer in the use of color to affect emotion and possesses the rare talent to see extremely subtle differences in color when looking at a paint chip.

Randy is known for his analytical approach to design, which he uses to guide clients through the creative process. He integrates their preferences, needs, and budget by combining his experience as an educator with his aptitude as a talented designer,

providing his customers with solutions that ultimately fulfills their desire for a beautiful home in which they will feel comfortable.

Hailing from a family of architects and engineers, as well as an aunt who was an interior designer, Gabberts' Nancy Woodhouse was genetically destined to be a designer herself. Her style is that of understated, casual elegance which reflects her clients' lifestyles and needs, a style she has been refining for over 20 years. "I try to help my clients achieve comfort with great style," she explains. "Our houses work for us, but they can also be functional and look wonderful at the same time." Nancy offers a total design solution to clients, comprehensively taking them through all stages of the creative process. The result is a home that is efficient and more livable.

Nancy likes to meet with clients in their homes where she asks a lot of questions and observes their lifestyles first-hand. The most successful projects are collaborative efforts between Nancy and her clients. "I always

ABOVE AND LEFT
Lion Mountain, Montana Residence
Jennifer Sheffert, Allied Member ASID,
Karen Soojian, ASID,
Karlene Hunter Baum, Allied Member ASID

LEFT Whitney Landmark Residence
Karen Soojian, ASID,
Karlene Hunter Baum, Allied Member ASID,
Sarah Bernardy, Allied Member ASID

BELOW LEFT Minneapolis Residence
Connie Wersal-LaVelle, Allied Member ASID

tell my clients that good design is a result of collaboration and focus," she notes. "The best clients follow the design process without involving outside, conflicting opinions." Nancy finds inspiration in her environment, whether she is at home or elsewhere. Through her travels, gardening, entertaining, and passion for the fine arts, she finds inspiration, keeping herself professionally motivated towards growth.

With a reputation for making homes more inviting, personal and comfortable, it is hard to believe that Gabberts started as a tire and appliance store in 1946. It was not too long after its more humble beginnings, that the Gabberts family converted their business into a home furnishings store, with furniture creatively displayed in vignettes—an industry "first"—allowing customers to envision how entire rooms would look and feel in their homes. Still owned and operated by the Gabberts family, the brand is rich with history, one that the designers continue to build upon by diligently bringing fresh, inventive home furnishing solutions to living spaces. ■

GABBERTS DESIGN STUDIO & FINE FURNISHINGS

3501 Galleria

Edina, MN 55435

Ph. 952-927-1500 Fax. 952-927-1555

www.gabberts.com

RIGHT North Oaks Residence
Karen Hodgdon, Allied Member ASID

BELOW Lion Mountain, Montana Residence
Jennifer Sheffert, Allied Member ASID,
Karen Soojian, ASID,
Karlene Hunter Baum, Allied Member ASID

Molly Gilbertson
Allied Member ASID

M. Gilbertson Design

M. GILBERTSON DESIGN

9072 Palmetto Drive

Eden Prairie, MN 55347

952-906-9628

mgg@mgilbertsondesign.com

LEFT This gourmet kitchen remodel juxtaposes the client's love of contemporary design with Mission styling using natural elements and color.

ABOVE This elegant bathroom uses frosted beach glass wall tile and Danby marble flooring which creates sophistication with a sense of serenity.

ABOVE RIGHT A stylishly designed infant room features custom cabinetry with a window seat for reading, and soft snuggly fabrics. A lime green and white wool rug softens the antique wood floor.

Molly Gilbertson is no stranger to "mixing it up" when it comes to her career in interior design. After graduating from the University of Minnesota with a four-year degree in interior design, Molly transitioned from doing commercial work at a large architectural firm to doing 75 percent residential and 25 percent commercial with her own firm. "Residential is so personal," she says. "You develop strong relationships with people because you are dealing with their homes—which should and do exemplify themselves."

Molly extends her creative diversity by enabling her clients to use color in pleasing and coordinated ways. "Design clients usually have a sense of what they like, but are often challenged in using color to actively define and accomplish it. A big part of my job, whether our intended result is to be subtle or bold, is to use color to evoke a positive mood or feeling about or reaction to the space. I free my clients from the prison of beige."

As for her style, Molly loves all of them, from historic to contemporary. Because design terminology means different things to different clients, Molly conducts a process called "visual listening" to uncover their likes and dislikes through photographs and magazine clippings. She then develops their ideal style using what she hears. It is her ability to translate the client's vision into actionable designs that has earned her the appreciation of a broad clientele, as well as numerous design awards. "In my view, it is not my personal style that is important to my clients. Instead, the outstanding designer should listen to the client and then bring out the client's own style in ways that are responsive to their unique needs for the space, creative, visually interesting, and sustainable."

Suzanne Goodwin, ASID, CID
Suzanne Goodwin & Associates

LEFT The Great Room in this Rancho Santa Fe home is rich in color, pattern, and texture.

ABOVE RIGHT The River Rock Fireplace in this Lake-side family room was the inspiration for the warm color palette of red, yellow, and grey-green.

While most people consult the Sears catalog to buy actual furniture, as a young girl, Suzanne Goodwin used it to design imaginary spaces. She would first draw rudimentary floor plans, and then, using the available items in the well-known resource, select drapery, lighting, bedding, furniture, and carpet to comprise in her fictitious home. "I spent hours designing and redesigning these spaces," she remembers. "I never dreamt that someday I would be doing the same thing in the real world with real clients."

This real world now consists of her own firm, Suzanne Goodwin & Associates, a single enterprise she started after several friends already established in the interior design business asked her to join their firm more than 20 years ago. Two associates and a host of independent contractors help her out with the accounting portion of the business and the CAD drawings, as needed, for various projects. With Suzanne Goodwin & Associates, Suzanne—now an ASID professional member, a CID in the State of Minnesota, a member of the ASID board of directors, an ASID president-elect, and a chairperson of the ASID Showcase House 2007 —has finished projects ranging from the formal traditional to the rustic informal to the soft comfortable contemporary in Minnesota, Colorado, California, and Florida. "As a Gemini, working with a broad spectrum of design suits my personality to a tee!" she exclaims.

Suzanne approaches each of her projects with the desire to understand her client's individuality so that she can reflect it in her designs. In turn, she appreciates a sense of humor and a proper perspective of the design process. To nurture this perspective, as well as determine the right style for her clients, Suzanne first conducts an informational interview, and shows them pictures of spaces that she has clipped from various magazines over the years.

She then often visits her clients' existing spaces to find out which items they would like to incorporate into the new design. She also makes sure their expectations are realistic when it comes to cost. For Suzanne's dream project, though, cost was not an issue, and neither was the client. This client not only had an unlimited budget, but was also nice and had great taste. "We—the client, architect, landscape designer, builder, and I—all worked great together," she explains. "What a treat it was!" By getting to know her clients' overall likes, wants, and needs, Suzanne has been able to create works worthy of publication in *Timber Home Magazine*, *Mpls. St. Paul Magazine*, *Lake Minnetonka Magazine*, and the *Minneapolis Star and Tribune*.

Also contributing to Suzanne's continued success is her affection for world travel. She has been to Italy, France, Great Britain, Portugal, Chile, Argentina, and Thailand, where she has found inspiration for many of her projects. She also frequently finds inspiration in her associates' work. "I am a rabid subscriber to design-oriented magazines, which feature great design work by my fellow interior designers," she says. At home, Suzanne finds balance in other artistic activities, including reading and needle-pointing, as well as in her expanding family's lives. ■

SUZANNE GOODWIN & ASSOCIATES

275 Market Street, Suite 517

Minneapolis, MN 55405

612-333-7717

suzannegoodwin@visi.com

FACING PAGE Rustic timbers, colored concrete floors, and rich leather furniture frame this lovely Colorado retreat.

ABOVE RIGHT Historical in every sense of the word, this guest suite combines traditional furnishings, fabrics, and colors in a most refreshing way.

RIGHT Slip-covered chairs, a rustic hand-hewed table, and a pulley chandelier all combine to give a quiet sophistication to this carriage house dining room.

Brandi Hagen, Allied Member ASID

Eminent Interior Design

In 2005, Brandi Hagen took the leap to start her own design firm, Eminent Interior Design, and hasn't looked back since. "I thought I could start out small and gradually grow my business, but the work just exploded from the start," Brandi said. Eminent, which means standing above others in quality, character, and reputation, is now staffed with one full-time office manager and two part-time design assistants who keep the business running smoothly, allowing Brandi to concentrate on her design strengths.

With the Eminent team, Brandi handles projects from residential interiors looking for a facelift to new construction and remodeling. She first gets to know her clients—most of them come from referrals—meets with all of the decision makers involved in the project, encouraging them to convey their likes and dislikes, and then creates an environment that suits their lifestyle. Throughout each project, Brandi works closely with local homeowners to select materials such as tile layouts, lighting, colors, and cabinetry design. "We make it easy for the different builders and tradespeople to work with us by providing spec sheets are easy to read and understand," she explains. "As a result, homes get built on time, and to the client's exact tastes."

Brandi preserves freshness in style while working on both contemporary and traditional projects. She refrains from creating a certain look, because it is important that her designs

LEFT This kitchen/family room addition maintains the character of the existing home while updating it for the flow of a modern family lifestyle.

ABOVE RIGHT The clients existing dining room underwent a face lift, creating an elegant yet comfortable dining experience that flows off of the family room.

ABOVE One side of twin vanities made from dark stained Mahogany topped with polished Pistachio Onyx. The vanity is complemented with a simple mirror and a mixture of Asian bronze and satin nickel finishes. *Photo courtesy of Trends Publishing International, Jamie Cobeldick.*

LEFT Mixing the clients contemporary taste with Asian heritage makes this master bath truly unique. Custom designed "Botanical Beach Grass" screen provides privacy and aesthetic appeal. *Photo courtesy of Trends Publishing International, Jamie Cobeldick.*

reflect her client's tastes. But this approach does not mean that her dream client would tell her to do whatever she wants to do. "My dream client is someone who has great style and taste, and asks me to pick up that style and taste and incorporate it into his or her home," she discloses. "It's harder to work with people who do not provide any input. I would rather work with someone who can say, 'this is how I envisioned my room,' and hires me to make that vision a reality."

Supporting Brandi's creative know-how is an education in interior design, and an internship she completed at William Beson Interior Design that led to 10 years as a designer with the firm. Brandi is an Allied ASID member, as well as a member of the National Association of Remodeling Industry (NARI), an active member of Junior League of Minneapolis, and a volunteer at Greater Minneapolis Crisis Nursery. Among her qualifications, it is her love for the work that keeps her designing, and it is her firm that enables her to carry out all types of projects. "Eminent is the right size to flexibly handle a range of small projects, and it is the right size to capably handle a range of large projects as well," she says. "It is the perfect place to be."

EMINENT INTERIOR DESIGN

6478 Westchester Circle

Minneapolis, MN 55427

612-767-1242 F: 612-767-1241

www.eminentid.com

ABOVE RIGHT Stone columns and exotic African wood floors in the living room complete a truly unique fusion of modern design and natural elements of this home.

RIGHT Stone hood, rift cut white oak cabinets, stainless steel wrapped island and exotic wood floors continue the nice use of modern design and natural elements

Kate Halverson, ASID, CID

Touch of Class Interiors

TOUCH OF CLASS INTERIORS

Minneapolis—Lake City

952-941-3023

612-201-4175 cell

toc@spacestar.net

www.tocinteriors.com

LEFT Lake Minnetonka Great Room—Memorable spaces consist of one of a kind *accents* and *color*. In this home, the custom area rug serves as the backdrop for a variety of seating options upholstered in fabrics with texture, color and durability. Classic comfort personified!

ABOVE RIGHT Hobby Rooms—This classic travel room is one you can dream in, work on a hobby, plan trips, arrange photographs, write poetry or paint yourself into your favorite *nesting space* to collect a multitude of memories. So much more than just another *decorated* room... *solace for the soul*.

"That which we elect to surround ourselves becomes the museum of our soul, an archive of our experiences," coined by Thomas Jefferson is one of Kate Halverson's mantras for new clients. "Surround yourselves with history, where you've been, what you treasure," Kate continues to advise as she assists clients with visualizing what they want their homes to reflect by asking them to choose five adjectives clarifying their interior goals. These adjectives become Halverson's roadmap for all her recommendations. "My job is getting them where they want to be, at home."

With a clear forecast, selections become easier and "I never repeat anything I've done for another client. There are so many delicious fabrics with distinctive patterns, texture and color, why would I ever replicate another client's choice?" Halverson specializes in creating one-of a kind custom designs, be it furniture, a painting, an area rug, wall finishes, "anything required to solve a problem," she adds. "More than anything, I want my clients' homes to be memorable with styles that stand the test of time. I love incorporating color," she adds, "and theme rooms based on a clients' hobbies or special interests, such as the classic travel room photographed. I've done rooms for train collectors, doll collectors, photographers, pilots, golfers; you name it."

Kate's approach to design—showcasing her clients' personalities and lives—is why Jefferson's quote is so appropriate. While Kate's talent for capturing her clients' dreams is what makes her successful, it is her ability to create stylish homes with soul that makes her work truly influential. ▪

Jean Hoffmann
ASID, CID
Chester-Hoffmann & Associates, Inc.

LEFT The brilliant use of colorful art and accessories creates a striking contrast to the spacious living area's deep monotone charcoal-and-white scheme in this St. Paul residence.

ABOVE RIGHT The foyer of this St. Paul residence is the epitome of tailored sophistication created by the use of shades of greys and blacks.

Jean Chester-Hoffmann discovered her love of design when her high school's curriculum required her to work as an intern in a field of her choice. Choosing interior design, she received the fortunate opportunity to learn about the trade for a summer at a design firm before she started college. Inspired by the internship, Jean ended up earning a degree in interior design and taking her knowledge to attain the position as an assistant to the principal of a large design firm in 1973. In 1976, she started designing independently and in 1989, she founded her present design firm, Chester-Hoffmann & Associates Incorporated, a small firm that handles residential and commercial projects. "We have used our distinguished style to design homes and offices throughout the United States for many prominent clients," she says. "Our clientele has included famed athletes, politicians, doctors, CEOs, and corporate principals of all ages, from those in their mid-twenties to those in their mid-eighties."

Clients are drawn to Jean's designs because of their tailored sophistication and her keen talent for blending beautiful and unusual fabrics, textures, and colors. She is also very approachable, even under the pressure of the most challenging design projects. In fact, the more challenging, the more determined she becomes to design spaces that inspire and reflect their owners. This determination has resulted in striking designs for a large warehouse

condominium conversion in Chicago, a ski lodge residence in Colorado, and a 15,000-square-foot residence in Northern Minnesota. Her dream project, though, is a carriage house conversion over a garage that bridges to the main residence. It has a two-story, vaulted gathering area with french doors, plaster textured walls, and a hand-scraped walnut floor. An open staircase leads to a balcony office over the garage, which has a large eyelash window overlooking Cedar Lake and the Downtown Minneapolis skyline. While this project is grand from a creative perspective, it is not the size that matters to Jean. "The projects that challenge my creative genius are my passion, no matter what the size," she remarks. "The clients who allow me to create receive my best design as an end result."

To thoroughly serve her clients, Jean believes that in addition to retaining a sense of creativity and flare for business, she must possess a background in psychology to understand them and actualize their needs. After she meets with her clients, visiting their existing space, she determines the design ideas that will work best for them. Next, she designs the space, selects colors, furnishings, fabrics, wall treatments, and window treatments, and then accessorizes to ultimately exceed their expectations.

ABOVE LEFT This master bedroom in colors of aubergine and apricot on a background palette of greys creates a tranquil backdrop for the painting "Ethnic Mother and Baby" by Jane Thompson.

LEFT The walls of this kitchen and informal dining area are surrounded by a natural textural hand-etched plaster design that defines clean, crisp simplicity.

As much as Jean appreciates and embraces her work and her clientele, her family's lives and their home always comes first. "My priority is to create a home that my loved ones personally enjoy and want to share with others," she says. As her most consistent "customers," she is constantly reinventing her definition of creativity to sustain such a place, but that is not a problem for Jean. "Knowledge is limited without creative imagination," she says, "because creativity encircles the world." ▪

CHESTER-HOFFMANN & ASSOCIATES, INC.

3948 W. 50th Street, Suite 204

Edina, MN 55424

952-925-9871

JCHAInc@aol.com

RIGHT The display of rich textures and design in shades of green and eggplant capture the inviting warmth and charm of this Sunfish Lake residence's vast two-and-a-half story vaulted great room.

BELOW Hand-painted clusters of French parrot tulips entwining a ribbon trellis create an elegant Country powder room.

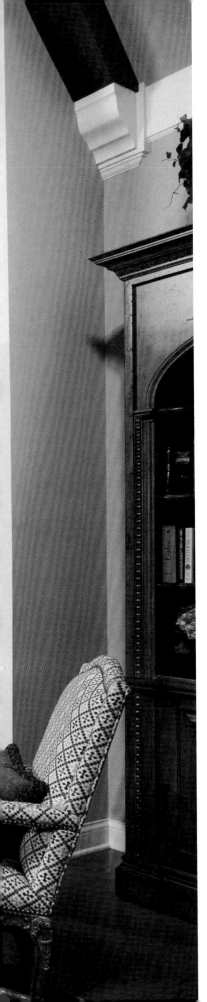

Susan Hoffman, ASID
DESIGNS!

LEFT L. Cramer luxury
home. Crosby Cove great
room. Designed by Susan
and Leah Fasching, ASID,
project manager.

ABOVE RIGHT Poolside
family room. Private
residence.

Founded and owned by Principal Designer Susan Hoffman, the Minneapolis firm DESIGNS! (a.k.a. Susan Hoffman Interior Designs, Inc.) is known for creating particularly relaxed and comfortable interiors with just the right mix of color and style. Susan is an honors graduate from Iowa State University and an ASID professional member. She passed the NCIDQ certification process in 1978 and served as the president of the ASID Minnesota Chapter from 1998 to 1999.

Over the last three decades, Susan has completed hundreds of design projects. Among the more unique or noteworthy projects has been a Montana ranch, a Caribbean sailboat and directing the interior renovation of the old Korbel Mansion in San Rafael, California. "I very much enjoy learning how tastes and methods of construction vary with different regions," she remarks. "It definitely keeps our jobs interesting." For her diverse work, she has earned numerous ASID awards, not to mention recognition in trade publications, such as *Midwest Home*, *Mpls. St. Paul Magazine*, *1001 Home Ideas* and *Audio Video Interiors*.

These days, Susan and her professional staff of five designers are focusing more and more on new construction. "Many clients appreciate the presence of a designer early in the homebuilding process," Susan explains. "We can make many selections and team with the

builder to ensure the homeowner has options, making the entire experience a positive one. In short, DESIGNS! plans, manages, designs and delivers a completed and coordinated look to new homes."

DESIGNS! also specializes in remodeling and renovation. In fact, Susan loves it; nothing excites her more than looking at an older home and envisioning what it might become. Moreover, she is popular for her ability to accessorize and finish a room, often using her reputable full-service, high-end retail accessory and furnishing store, P.O.S.H. (Property of Susan Hoffman) to do so. Susan established P.O.S.H.—named after the stamp that appeared on luxury liner passenger luggage in the 18th century— to provide customers with furniture and home accessories. "With the store, I can make the entire design experience easier and more complete for clients," says Susan.

To further serve her clients as competently as possible, Susan stays in touch with new ideas and consumer demands by attending furniture markets, monitoring design publications and meeting with sales representatives in the industry. Separating her from her competitors is her desire for natural, organic materials and her background for working with the region's top builders. As a result, her clients receive unique service versus trite trendiness because they are involved in the design evolution. "It is important for us to direct our clients within the parameters of quality design," Susan says. "We work closely with them to create an environment that meets their functional, aesthetic and safety needs. The design plan that develops is a comprehensive approach that makes the ultimate result more satisfying."

DESIGNS!

317 E. Wayzata Blvd.

Wayzata, MN 55391

952-475-0196

susan@susanhoffman.com

ABOVE RIGHT L. Cramer luxury home. Medina. Designed by Susan and Leah Fasching, ASID, project manager.

RIGHT Orono living room. Private residence.

Kathryn Johnson, Allied Member ASID

Kathryn Johnson Interiors

KATHRYN JOHNSON
INTERIORS

4205 Minnesota Lane N.

Plymouth, MN 55446

763-208-4202

kathryn@kjinteriorsinc.com

LEFT AND ABOVE RIGHT
Designing with the colors
in your life.

A designer for 25 years, Kathryn owns and operates Kathryn Johnson Interiors Inc. Kathryn does not only have her BS degree in art, but is also a firm believer in continuing education. Feeling that it is every professional's responsibility to continuously update their industry knowledge, is why you will find her at one of the major furniture markets at least once a year or perusing the latest fashions at kitchen and bath shows. Having been published in *Window Fashions Magazine* and numerous local shelter magazines, she knows the value of sharing ideas with her peers and the public.

When clients meet Kathryn, they are often pleased with her enthusiasm. She includes them in the design process by explaining to them that it is her job to expand their horizons and keep them on track. "Our industry has all the magical ingredients to make peoples lives more beautiful, more functional and even more secure. The sky is the limit, but not their budgets. Sometimes, this is like taking a child to Walt Disney World for only two hours and giving them two dollars in spending money," she jokes. Kathryn's an optimist and believes that reality doesn't need to be painful. She works with her clients to discover creative solutions that deliver fabulous end results, all within a budget. Her main objective is having her clients confident in the fact that their new interiors have become all that they could be.

Kathryn has a specific talent for providing a proper perspective on the goal. "I advise my clients, 'Good design is a wise investment. Poor design never stops costing you money.'" In the end, she very much enjoys seeing her clients' contentment and satisfaction with the results.

While traveling and fine art inspires her, she still nurtures her creative abilities by sketching and painting. To keep life in perspective she enjoys a good game of golf. ■

Janis Kennedy
Allied Member ASID

J. Roux Interior Design, Inc.

Interior design is in Janis Kennedy's blood. So much so that she designed and selected all of the finishes for the home her parents bought for her family when she was 14 years old. "I can see projects in my head," she says. "I realized I could when I started designing imaginary interiors using items from the Sears catalog as a kid." Now 22 years into her career, Janis is with J. Roux Interior Design, an esteemed full-service studio partly known for its 14,000-square-foot showroom from which clients can choose their ideal materials among the most current selection available.

Retaining an expert staff of four designers educated and degreed in interior design, J. Roux Interior Design has been featured on HGTV's "Passport to Design," a television program that shows viewers how to make over spaces in their homes using cultural and international themes, on Discovery Home, and in many magazines. Janis and the other ASID Allied Members of J. Roux have also been featured in the "Who's Who" of design and in the ASID Showcase Home tour for three years. Furthermore, Janis and her J. Roux colleagues have worked on homes for the Street of Dreams, the renowned show tour that features a collection of fully furnished and accessorized custom show homes on a single street in exclusive developments around the United States. They have also collaborated on five luxury homes for the Luxury Home Tour, receiving recognition for designing homes that reflect the imagination

ABOVE A transitional, all-season porch with a feminine flair that features a stone fireplace, wicker chairs, capstone coffee tables, and an antique Soumak rug.

of the country's premier builders. Additionally, the J. Roux team has worked on homes for the spring and fall seasons of the Parade of Homes tour, hosted by the Builders Association of the Twin Cities. In fact, the design firm has showcased at least one home per season on the tour for the last 10 years.

With J. Roux, Janis not only works on furnishings, but also on all construction layouts and every detail that homes require. In the area of new construction, she knows that even if her clients are extremely knowledgeable when it comes to building a new home, it can still be overwhelming. So Janis and the rest of the J. Roux Interior Design group use their expertise in building to handle the initial planning, selection process, and time management associated with the project, so clients do not have to deal with its complexities. To implement the new construction process, Janis first reviews

A four-poster bed dressed with silk bedding, handmade carpeting with a unique floral pattern and Regency silk benches create an inviting master retreat.

her clients' blueprints for aesthetics, function, adequate space allocation, and floor plan design. She then walks her clients through selecting the right plumbing, lighting, and flooring to ultimately create for them the most customized homes possible, while making sure that she carefully considers every detail involved.

As for her perspective on style, Janis is firm in her belief that quality designers do not design with just one. "I strongly feel that we successfully get into our clients' heads and create distinct environments that express their relative desires and tastes," she asserts. "We care about every project as if it were our own home." Taking this measure still creates a sensation of excitement for Janis, because it presents a new experience with each client. After 22 years, she maintains that every project is just as thrilling as her first.

Janis starts projects with the goal to comprehensively identify what her clients are looking for in regards to interior design. So she meets with them in the comfort of their own homes, observes their lifestyles first-hand, and takes note of how they use their spaces. "This tells me more about a client than anything else," Janis explains. She then places herself in the mindset that she is creating a lifestyle for her clients that will enhance the quality of their lives and giving them an environment for nurturing their families as well as their souls. With such philosophy, Janis was able to auspiciously create a French-inspired home for a client who gave her carte blanche to handle every stage of the design process, from selecting the builder to determining the landscaping. The result was an authentic abode complete with antique wood floors and antique stone flooring dug up out of a Basilica in France; a genuine environment notably fulfilling for her client.

While she found the creative process involved with this project particularly inspiring because it presented a new adventure from task to task, Janis finds everyday inspiration in everything she touches, sees, and hears during a design project. When she is not designing, she finds enjoyment in gardening, reading, and relaxing, and, most of all, in retaining an appreciation for life.

J. ROUX INTERIOR DESIGN, INC.

3555 Holly Lane North, Suite 20

Plymouth, MN 55447

763-560-8689

BELOW A family room off the children's wing emphasizes comfort and durability, accentuated by a vaulted ceiling, hand-painted to mimic the sky.

BELOW LEFT Expansive windows provide optimal garden views and emphasize scale with a vaulted ceiling, hand-timbered beams and hand-tufted rugs.

Dea L'Heureux, ASID

Dea L'Heureux Interiors

DEA L'HEUREUX INTERIORS

275 Market Street, Suite 548

Minneapolis, MN 55405

612-673-0515

deaphil@hotmail.com

LEFT The client envisioned a bright, light living room with clear colors. The result was just what the client wished for. A truly eclectic, lively room designed with a combination of antiques, custom-made pieces and a stunning custom area rug.

ABOVE RIGHT Perfect for cozy dinners and inviting conversations, this classic dining room reflects understated comfort. The George III Hepplewhite chairs harmonize with the antique Chinese screen and Persian rug.

Combining traditional European design with contemporary vitality is the hallmark of interior designer Dea L'Heureux, who brings a wealth of knowledge to her interior design projects. Born and raised in Europe in an artistic family, it was only natural that she chose interior design as a profession. "I enjoy coming up with creative ideas and innovative design solutions for all my clients. It's important to listen to what they want, to see what they have, and what they want to incorporate," she says. "Through this process, I've developed very personal and long-standing relationships with my clients."

After receiving her degree in art from the University of Minnesota, Dea accepted an internship with one of the area's renowned interior design studios, eventually becoming the assistant to the firm's senior designer. Drawing upon her vast experience, she established her Minneapolis-based company, Dea L'Heureux Interiors in 1981, and it has been thriving ever since.

Over the years, Dea has designed exceptional rooms, all which received media attention, were featured in various magazines, and received a number of industry awards. In addition to her design work, Dea has appeared on television discussion panels, as well as volunteered her time to judging student design projects, lectured on interior design, and worked with many charities. "It's always my hope that my interiors reflect the successful relationship between myself and my clients' wishes," she says.

John Lassila, Allied Member ASID

John Lassila & Associates

LEFT Colorful Asian influence accessories and art offer an exotic flavor to this transitional condominium living area.

ABOVE RIGHT Rich wood finishes balance the bright color palette used in this dining area. Original art and an Italian art glass chandelier add sophistication.

As the only interior designer on the John Lassila and Associates staff, John Lassila closely adheres to the design process and always sustains interaction with clients. He starts projects by talking with clients at length about their lifestyle, covering topics such as how they entertain, how they interact with their friends and family, where they travel, and how they conduct themselves in their living spaces. Maintaining a close relationship with his clients as the design process continues, John encourages them to freely express themselves and then uses this expression in the designs he creates. "I can picture spaces completely finished, so I am able to efficiently help clients work toward the final goal," he explains. "To reflect their tastes, I personalize interiors by using their own artifacts and collectibles." Further personalizing his projects is a varying group of tradesmen, artisans, and contractors. With their support, he is able to continually get excited about the endless number of possibilities he can carry out as a designer. Different materials and resources comprise these possibilities, so no combination is ever the same, which results in newness and freshness for every project.

John Lassila and Associates is a full-service studio specializing in residential design. The design firm offers remodeling and new construction consultation, and handles many types of projects, from country houses, vacation houses, and lake houses, to

primary residences and condominiums. Depending on clients' needs, John Lassila and Associates is adept at providing design using existing furniture, home office design, selection of interior finishes, and window and wall treatments, in addition to new construction and remodels, renovation, and coordination. He also designs media rooms, handles projects within the restaurant, club, and hospitality industries, and provides a shopping service.

A member of International Market Square, John retains immediate access to an abundance of quality furnishings from more than 1,500 manufacturers, most of which are not readily available through local retail merchants. No matter what his clients' desires are in furniture, upholstery pieces, fabrics, textiles, floor and wall coverings, accessories, antiques, art, lighting, or outdoor living, John can fulfill them, quickly and completely. His International Market Square membership also enables him to find building products, such as home theater items, flooring and

ABOVE LEFT A monochromatic yet warm color scheme unifies a mix of furniture styles in this lower level entertainment room.

LEFT Contemporary art and lighting update the look of classic traditional furnishings in this living room. A French-made carpet inspired the color palette.

tile, entry doors and door hardware, and landscape products. For his office and hospitality creations, John can use International Market Square's availability to create every look from executive furnishings to work stations, seating, commercial-grade fabric and wall coverings, art, lighting, and interior and exterior landscape products.

If John were to pick a couple of his favorite projects that other designers have completed around Minneapolis, he would choose Roger Beck Florist and Circa Gallery. These favorites very much reflect the stylistic range John likes to use in his own designs. He particularly appreciates Roger Beck Florist, a floral boutique in trendy and gentrified uptown Minneapolis, for its elegant yet understated design. He likes Circa Gallery, an art gallery near Loring Park at the edge of downtown Minneapolis, for its overall embodiment of contemporary style. Featuring a broad variety of media, including painting, mixed media, and graphics, the gallery's mission is to provide an awareness and appreciation of contemporary styles and expressions, which is an effort that John absolutely embraces, professionally and personally.

RIGHT Custom-cast glass used to fabricate the vanity and shower surround lightens this contemporary master bath. Classic travertine tile adds warmth.

Architectural Antiques in northeast Minneapolis, a business that sells rescued architectural artifacts, is another one of John's favorites not because of its interior design, but because of its comprehensive collection of antique architectural elements. John frequents Architectural Antiques for its vintage lighting, doors and windows, yard and garden products, mantles and cabinetry, original hardware, and ecclesiastical artifacts to complement his clients' existing pieces, transforming a room or building into an environment of beauty and harmony.

Ever since starting his firm 10 years ago—after previously working with several larger interior design firms for more than 10 years—John has found most of his inspiration in his clients. "When I help clients create nurturing spaces, they take the positive energy they derive from these spaces out into the world," he says. "They feel good, so they make others feel good, which is an inspiration to me." John also loves to work on his own home, experimenting with ideas he often applies to other projects. In addition to finding enjoyment in such experimentation, John also loves to go to the opera, entertain, cook, travel, and read, leisure activities that enhance his ability to conceive of and implement the newness and freshness he is known for conveying in his work. ◼

LEFT An earthy color palette inspired by the room's original stone walls contrasts with ebony cabinetry and high-sheen granite in this bar area.

ABOVE Deep aubergine walls and luxurious fabrics create a dramatic atmosphere in this dining room.

JOHN LASSILA & ASSOCIATES

275 Market Street, Suite 299

Minneapolis, MN 55405

612-672-9959 F: 612-672-9692

lassila@visi.com

Emily Little
Allied Member ASID

Valcucine Minneapolis

VALCUCINE MINNEAPOLIS

275 Market Street, Suite 145

Minneapolis, MN 55405-1627

612-341-4588 F: 612-341-4589

emily@valcucinempls.com

LEFT Valcucine Ricicla cabinets in European cherry. Custom home in Chanhassen, MN.

ABOVE Valcucine Free Play cabinets in matt lacquer. Renovation in Minnetonka, MN.

ABOVE RIGHT Valcucine Artematica cabinets in Dark Oak with horizonatal grain. Custom home on Cedar Lake in Minneapolis, MN.

Having graduated with a bachelor of architecture from Iowa State University, it is no wonder why Emily Little's style of design is a fusion between beauty and mathematics. She designs kitchens with aesthetics and function in mind, making scale, geometry, spatial proportion and the client's needs a priority. Emily is particularly drawn to the importance of a design's details, big and small. "I like the process of creating design based on my client's specific situation," she says. "Rather than doing what they have done before, what their neighbors have done, or what they saw on HGTV, I love clients who are not afraid to be themselves."

Emily's firm specializes in using the Valcucine brand Italian kitchen system cabinetry because of its aesthetics, quality, innovation, materials, non-toxicity and environmentally-friendly aspects. "We're a small company with big ideas and huge innovation," she notes. "Valcucine has been a world leader in promoting green initiatives in the kitchen and furniture industry since 1980." A pioneer herself, Emily has been published in *Midwest Home and Garden*, *METRO Magazine* and *Mpls. St. Paul Magazine* for her attention to beauty, ergonomics and green design. Emily is a member of the U.S. Green Building Council, and furthermore, she is helping to lay the foundation for a Green Committee in the ASID Minnesota Chapter, while studying to earn Leadership in Energy and Environmental Design (LEED) certification.

Emily often works in collaboration with another designer or architect rather than as the sole designer, which she prefers. "I enjoy being a part of a larger team," she remarks. "Especially when everyone's ultimate goal is for a client to never wish the space was another way."

Karen Lund, Allied Member ASID
& Marie Schlink, ASID

The Two of Us Interiors

THE TWO OF US INTERIORS

275 Market Street, Suite 272

Minneapolis, MN 55405

612-373-0590

thetwoofusims@msn.com

LEFT Soft colors make this award-winning sitting room a refreshing retreat. Filled with Gustavian Swedish furniture, the room has an authentic old-world charm.

ABOVE Titled "The Enchanted Castle," this award-winning four-year-old boy's room evokes visions of Camelot and the legendary King Arthur and his knights.

ABOVE RIGHT A closet in a sunny porch off the boy's bedroom was transformed into a small curtained stage for him to portray his legendary characters.

The Two of Us Interiors' Karen Lund and Marie Schlink design under the philosophy that a well-designed space is warm, gracious, and inviting; reflects the owners' personality and interests; functions efficiently; enhances human relationships; lifts spirits; and is timeless yet evolving. Not a tall order for two women who have been in business together since 1984, having initially discovered their love for the process of design while decorating dollhouses as children. At the beginning of their careers, they worked in the hospitality field—they designed a historic inn, restaurant and motel, retirement community, and offices—but today, they primarily focus on residential projects. "Working as a team is unique," Karen says. "Our clients seem to enjoy this approach and it provides a good balance, since we try to avoid letting our personal tastes get in the way of what our clients like and want." As a result, the two have earned three ASID Showcase House People's Choice Awards from *Mpls. St. Paul Magazine*, a first place award at the MN Chapter ASID 2002 Design Competition, and the Trillium Award from the Builders Association of the Twin Cities.

Clients choose the talent of The Two of Us Interiors when they want a warm and gracious style. Inspired by nature—from the grandeur of mountains to the detail of a seashell —Karen and Marie are very detail-oriented visually and love to accessorize, especially with their clients own meaningful collectibles. "Because of our sensitivity to environmental issues, we encourage clients to use existing furnishings when possible," Marie explains. "Doing so also adds character and makes the space especially theirs." ▪

Macy's Interior Design Studios

People all over the world are familiar with the department store chain Macy's. Since 1858, when Rowland Hussey Macy opened its predecessor, a "fancy dry foods" store in New York City called R.H. Macy & Co., Macy's has come a long way. The acclaimed chain now offers discerning shoppers in 45 U.S. states, the District of Columbia, Puerto Rico, and Guam popular fashion and affordable luxury at more than 400 stores. Reflecting its evolved sense for style and spirit is the retailer's full-service design studio, Macy's Interior Design Studio, in the Minneapolis/St. Paul area. The design studio offers a highly trained, degreed staff of professional interior designers who guide clients through the design process, helping them to create interiors that accommodate and impress. There are 30 senior designers who work for Macy's Interior Design Studio at a total of three locations in the Minneapolis/St. Paul area, with experience ranging from five years to more than 30 years in the business.

As a full-service studio, Macy's Interior Design Studio offers a wide range of manufacturers to thoroughly service clients' needs, such as Baker, Henredon, Sherrill, Swaim, Bernhardt, Hickory Chair, American Leather, W. Shellig, and Natuzzi. To further convenience clients, the designers with the studio can also access the Design Mart for additional manufacturers, fabric houses, and accessory lines difficult to find anywhere else.

When serving clients—for the initial meeting, customers can set up a consultation with a designer at Macy's in-store studio or, if preferred, in their home—Macy's Interior Design Studio's interior designers commit to complementing their unique tastes and lifestyles. The professionals team with clients to realize their visions and then combine these clients' personal style with their own proficient knowledge and state-of-the-art design ideas. The result: a beautifully restored bathroom, a more open and airy kitchen, or a modernized living room. With Macy's Interior Design Studio, the design possibilities are endless.

Macy's Interior Design Studio's designers not only help clients make the right decisions for their home, but they are also notably adept with project management for new construction as well as remodel projects, retaining extensive experience with every category of home furnishings and furniture, window and wall treatments,

LEFT This European traditional home combines classic architectural details with comfortable furnishings in a warm and gracious palette.

floor coverings, art, lighting, art consultancy, and accessories. Such capability enables the studio's designers to provide expert assistance while offering the best in fresh ideas, innovative floor plans, personalized color schemes, customized furniture, and home accessory. Services are complimentary when purchases are made through the design studio. Some consultation services require an hourly fee.

Extending its breadth, Macy's Interior Design Studio proudly features an annual Trend House in its Edina store, which showcases the latest in home fashion trends. Trend House is an actual house inside the store; furnished and decorated on the cutting edge of interior design. Originated in 1937 at the Chicago State Street location, because many customers naturally stopped spending money on decorating their homes due to the Depression, Trend House was developed to reveal creativity while decorating on a budget. In those days, the

RIGHT Macy's designers select beautiful artwork, area rugs and accessories to complement and complete every space.

decorators who worked on Trend House built two houses—one modern style and one Victorian—and placed them side by side to show customers how to put furniture together in room settings. In recent years, Trend House has reflected the latest trends in furnishings and decor, featuring styles such as, and as different as, a penthouse suite and a French country retreat.

For its designers' praiseworthy work, Macy's Interior Design Studio has been published in numerous home fashion magazines and local community publications. It has also been awarded for its room designs and window treatments, reflecting the great quality that the Macy's name has meant to many for close to a century and a half. ■

ABOVE LEFT Theatrically draped windows, the focal point of the room, set the stage for spectacular lake views.

LEFT The dramatic tension between classical and contemporary creates a dynamic interior space that confidently combines the best of the past with the excitement of the future.

Edina location:

7235 France Avenue South

Edina, MN 55435

952-896-2160

Minneapolis location:

700 On The Mall

Minneapolis, MN 55402

612-375-2491

Rosedale location:

1375 Commerce Street

Roseville, MN 55113

651-639-2040

RIGHT Gorgeous and glorious, this dining room is the luxurious jewel of the prestigious Summit Avenue turn of the century mansion.

Sandra Mangel, ASID, CID
Sandra Mangel Interior Design

LEFT Leather bound sisal area rug defines this multi functional space in this Lake of the Isles residence. Subtle Asian influence, monochromatic scheme, natural fibers and materials support the serine classic simplicity of this gathering room.

ABOVE RIGHT Custom designed iron and glass, granite fireplace surround and cherry entertainment center complements adjacent Kitchen not shown.

Sandra Mangel was president of the Minnesota Chapter of American Society of Interior Designers (ASID) in 2004 and in 2006, ASID honored her with the prestigious Designer of Distinction award. Sandra and her mother, Eleanor Mady established Two's Company, a retail gift and accessory boutique and interior design studio in 1974. In 2004, the retail aspect of the business was eliminated to allow space for a client presentation area with a living room setting to showcase her work. With the help of her loyal team, project manager Nicole Crow, draftsperson Julie Nordine, and design assistant Katie Erickson, Sandra is privileged to accommodate her clients not only in Minnesota, but coast to coast.

Sandra attributes her success to her mother's influence. A great lady of style, Eleanor, an accomplished seamstress, designed and made Sandra's clothes as well as her own. She instilled in her daughter a discerning eye for quality and a love for beautiful fabrics. It's a characteristic that is apparent in Sandra's stellar attention to dressmaker detail in her elegant drapery designs and upholstery treatments.

Sandra travels extensively worldwide, as well as shops the major design venues throughout the country to bring to her clients fresh and exciting resources. Though she hesitates to label her design style, she says "versatile, we're not cookie-cutter, nor a one-size fits all." If she does have an underlying theme, it is classic, timeless, comfortable, appropriate and

inviting. Our current projects include several modern city loft and condo spaces where form, line, texture and choice of sustainable materials takes precedence, suburban new construction where the emphasis on luxury is paramount, and urban remodels where sensitivity and adherence to the architectural history of the home is relevant.

On the onset of a new project, she listens to her client's desires, takings her cues from their existing environment, lifestyles, and personal tastes. "You have to understand who you are designing for," she says. She is excited about the trend toward remodeling in lieu of relocating, and is busy creating master suites from adjacent rooms, adding family rooms, expanding and renovating kitchens, converting basements and attics into more usable spaces. "I enjoy working with space," she notes. Her team has the experience and expertise to manage a commission from beginning to end. Regardless of the scope of the project, her approach and attentiveness is consistent.

ABOVE LEFT A warm comfortable collected look in this Cedar Lake living room, features an eclectic mix of period styles, patterns and rich textures.

LEFT This Edina residence kitchen with walkout deck for a family of eight with maximized storage. 48" Viking range, two dishwashers, computer desk and floor to ceiling pantry not visible.

Sandra figures prominently in the design community, and her outstanding work has won her numerous ASID awards in both commercial and residential categories. Additionally, her projects have been featured in many local and national publications.

Sandra loves the quote "Beauty is the promise of happiness." She believes it implies order. "It's about attitude and what we are attracted to internally, we seek what is intrinsically good, striving to attain a balance in our lives," she says. "It's a privilege to work in a profession that has a positive effect on people's lives."

SANDRA MANGEL INTERIOR DESIGN

4601 Bryant Avenue South

Minneapolis, MN 55409

612-827-5395 F: 612-827-7365

sandramangel@hotmail.com

www.sandramangel.com

BELOW AND RIGHT Eden Prairie luxurious spa master bath incorporates mosaic inlays, frameless shower, crystal chandelier and sconces. Under vanity lighting and in floor radiant heat, combine to enhance this elegant space.

Sandy Monson, ASID, CID
Lynn Monson, ASID, CID CKD, CBD

Monson Interior Design

MONSON INTERIOR DESIGN

Minneapolis, MN

612-338-0665

monson@visi.com

LEFT Kitchen cabinetry embellishments—moldings, spindles, corbels—are details worthy of the elegant 1910 home. Upper cabinets fronted with stained glass doors are lit from within.

ABOVE The striking textural combination of granite, maple and cherry woods, and copper comes to life in the abundant natural light of this two-story kitchen.

ABOVE RIGHT This semi-circular library doubling as an office is an expression of the client's appreciation for beautiful woods of rich and unusual grain.

Lynn and Sandy Monson have been synchronically—and successfully—combining their talents for high-end kitchen and bath design out of their two-person studio for more than 25 years. Their firm, Monson Interior Design, has received widespread recognition for the couple's varied designs, such as the eclectic new kitchen they designed in a large old home on the shores of one of Minneapolis' city lakes. "The new kitchen was actually carved out of a warren of rooms that had been back-of-the-house servant quarters under and behind the central grand staircase," Lynn describes.

Lynn and Sandy are both professional ASID members and Certified Interior Designers, and Lynn is CKD and CBD-certified through NKBA, and holds a residential building contractor license. Together, they offer total design and project management in a design-build format, which has earned them numerous state and national design awards from the National Kitchen and Bath Association and the American Society of Interior Designers.

The couple welcomes partnerships with others in the industry, often teaming with designers who call them into projects for their kitchen and bath specialization and contracting. It is this enthusiastic synergy that clients see, as well as their emphasis on listening. "Every project is collaboration, whether with other professionals or directly with the clients, and listening is the way to discover how they want the space to look and feel as well as function," explains Sandy. "We help our clients discover and creatively express their own personal styles within the parameters of good design."

Jim Noble
Allied Member ASID
Noble Interiors Inc.

LEFT An Antique Sorouk rug anchors this monochromatic living room. The neutral palette allows the client's collection of important Asian accessories and original art to become the focus of this restful room.

ABOVE RIGHT Strong wall color in this sun-drenched room coupled with interesting furniture make this room cheerful and refreshing.

Jim Noble creates ideal spaces for his clients with many philosophies in mind. While working with them, his mentality is, "Do unto others as you would have them do unto you." While planning spaces, he embraces the credo that every room should have the imprint of the homeowner. And while implementing design, he believes that art and accessories make the room a home and "Life is short. You had better surround yourself with pretty things and lots of love." As for the end result, Jim reasons that, "Your rooms should speak volumes about you even when you are not there!" In the case of one home, Jim just learned that this last philosophy has particularly rung true considering its homeowner passed away three years ago and her family estate is still placing orders.

Jim started Noble Interiors in 1997 having had already worked in the interior design field for 20 years and with a bachelor of arts from the University of St. Thomas in St. Paul. Supported by an administrative manager, drafting professionals, and other trade experts that vary from project to project, Jim creates soft-traditional interiors that are inviting, warm, comfortable, and feature touches of humor. "I create elegance without the priss," he remarks. "I do not follow trends." More of a custom designer, Jim uncovers his clients' specific needs by first talking with them on the phone and then meeting with them in person at no charge. He listens carefully, asks many questions, and then listens some more, guaranteeing that they get what they want. This approach pertains to not only residential projects, but commercial projects as well. From dental offices to churches and funeral homes, Jim lends his tasteful and sophisticated designs to projects of many calibers.

To continually create the beautifully distinctive interiors for which he is known, the ASID member looks to the work of widely celebrated decorators—past and present—his travels, coffee table books, nature, architecture, and lifestyle magazines for inspiration. For his work, he has been published in the *Minneapolis Star Tribune*, *Edina Magazine*, and *Mpls. St. Paul*. The full-page article in the *Minneapolis Star Tribune* covered his own home, a 120-year-old Federal Revival-style house in Minneapolis, and his family, a wife of 23 years, five children, and a poodle named Riley. Jim's home flaunts a palette of golds and greens with touches of red against a neutral backdrop to maintain a bright and upbeat atmosphere. A showcase of his talent, it is somewhat eclectic with traditional English style that integrates Asian and French influences, creating a formal, but comfortable environment.

Jim is a Certified Kitchen and Bath Remodeler through the National Association of the Remodeling Industry, but he considers his marriage certificate his greatest "certification." A true family man, he beams about his profession, but he lives for his family. "They are my interests," he says.

NOBLE INTERIORS INC.

20 E. Elmwood Place

Minneapolis, MN 55419

612-904-0933 F: 612-904-0932

jnoble@nobleinteriorsinc.com

www.nobleinteriorsinc.com

ABOVE RIGHT Shades of beige and comfortable antiques counterpoint the clients significant, colorful contemporary art collection.

RIGHT This once contemporary bath room now reflects the homeowners love of fine French living.

SMILEY GLOTTER NYBERG
ARCHITECTS, INC.

111 Washington Avenue
North, Suite 300
Minneapolis, MN 55401
612-332-1401
mail@sgnarchitects.com

LEFT Entry and lobby of Tradition Capital Bank in Edina, Minnesota. Building on a concept of customer friendly spaces where the banker transacts business with the customer in a comfortable, residential setting.

ABOVE The Conference room is furnished in a warm transitional style, yet with all the current electronic conveniences. Gary also selected the artwork and accessories, the original tapestry in the buffet niche was designed to follow its arched top.

ABOVE RIGHT The bank overlooks the lake and fountain at Centennial Lakes as seen from the "Dining Room" customer contact area. Beyond the open door is a view into the "Living Room" area.

Gary Nyberg, ASID
Smiley Glotter Nyberg Architects, Inc.

Fascinated by spaces and intrigued by possibilities, Gary Nyberg has been interested in architecture and interior design for as long as he can remember. "My parents tell me that my first drawings looked a lot like houses," he says. Now 35 years into his career, Gary is the respected president of the over-80-year-old firm Smiley Glotter Nyberg Architects, Inc., where he oversees a talented team of designers, planners, and construction technicians.

Perhaps Gary's greatest asset is his ability to visualize and materialize. In other words, he can find the "good bones" of a building, visualize its potential, and turn it into a great space. One tactic he is known for using to fulfill such potential is revolving his designs around a favorite painting, piece of furniture, or collection. "I then use color to add warmth to the space, as well as create texture and a bit of whimsy for fun," he explains. "Mies van der Rohe said it best... 'God is in the details.'"

To determine the right details, Gary first listens and observes his clients, and then asks them many questions. This approach has led to three ASID awards for the design work he did for First Bank Systems, as well as ASID awards for United Hospital and the College of St. Catherine. "Many of the design concepts that we developed for First Bank Systems, such as personal customer contact areas, were utilized by Tradition Capital Bank because they paralleled their vision of private banking services," he shares. When design ideas spread from a client to a competitor, you know the designer has mastered his trade. Gary is this designer.

Martha O'Hara Interiors

Beret Evenstad, Allied Member ASID, Annie Graunke, Allied Member ASID & Laura Peck, Allied Member ASID

When clients work with Martha O'Hara Interiors they benefit from a creative interplay among its 10 interior designers, since each designer can contribute a different style and varied tastes to the project. In addition, because of the firm's size, there is always a designer available to service the client and various design resources are easily accessible. Five senior designers Martha O'Hara, Mary Adams, Carrie Kirby, Chris Weiss, and Kathy Carter Wray each have 15 to 20 years of interior design experience. They are joined by newer designers who are all Allied Members of ASID, Beret Evenstad, Annie Graunke and Laura Peck and by design assistants Darsi Floersch and Jayme Osterdyk. The firm's founder, Martha O'Hara, started Martha O'Hara Interiors with MBA and CPA credentials, giving the firm the ability to handle each project as its own small business. Accordingly, the firm services clients from the beginning of a project to its very last detail while heeding a determined budget. "We decide on a detailed budget upfront to reduce the anxiety that numbers can cause," she explains. "This way, our clients can truly enjoy the design process."

Beret Evenstad started designing when she went back to school for a second degree in interior design and remodeled her own home. Beret treats her clients' homes much like she has her own, designing them to reflect their stories while synonymously making their home's interiors comfortable, personal, and gracious. This is not to say that her style is conservative; contrarily, she loves spaces that elicit the coveted "Wow!" factor, where people feel their impact immediately upon walking into them. "I love it when a space makes me notice it," she says. "I design a room so people see its beauty without thinking it looks overdone."

Annie Graunke classifies her style as eclectic and relaxed. She often uses an antique piece or a family heirloom to give transitional/contemporary rooms more interest. "I enjoy mixing pattern, color, and texture to create a casual feel," she says. To achieve this look, Annie draws on the inspiration she gets from natural materials, such as sisal and other woven textiles, and nature's elements, such as the color cerulean in a clear sky or the color spring green in fresh grass.

When Annie first starts working with clients, she likes to get them excited about the project by sharing her ideas for each space. Then to tailor her style to their specific home, she translates their needs and thoughts into creative and workable designs. When she has completed the design work, she presents it to the client. Over her career, Annie has discovered that she especially enjoys working with clients who completely trust her. "One of my clients gave me free reign in their guestroom and it turned out to be their favorite room in the house," she comments. "Not many clients are able to do that, so I cherish those who can!"

Similarly, Martha O'Hara Interiors' Laura Peck's dream client trusts in her design abilities, and possesses a willingness to pursue unconventional designs for unexpected, fabulous results. Such willingness is essential for her to successfully fulfill her individual

ABOVE RIGHT AND RIGHT Exotic, authentic Polynesian dining in a casual home on a Hawaii golf course.

style of design: truly eclectic. Laura loves soft contemporary, clean-lined furnishings, but what distinguishes her from other designers is that she likes to add an element of drama with an unexpected piece. "My philosophy on design is that it is subjective," she remarks. "If you know your client, it is OK to break the rules to create an atmosphere that is truly unique to them." While her education in textiles and consumer services at the University of North Dakota taught her how to become a professional and develop her standout sense of style, Laura attributes her career to her innate creativity. She believes that her ability is a gift that comes from within and that the world is a clean slate just waiting for personal color.

By creating beauty without exploiting design, the designers of Martha O'Hara Interiors have earned several regional and national interior design awards. Separately, each designer possesses her own flare, but together, they are a flame that illuminates every project they touch.

MARTHA O'HARA INTERIORS

8353 Excelsior Boulevard

Hopkins, MN 55343

952-908-3150 F: 952-908-3153

info@oharainteriors.com

www.oharainteriors.com

BELOW Skyline vistas in a Manhattan master suite.

Gigi Olive, ASID, CID

Gigi Olive Interiors, LLC

GIGI OLIVE INTERIORS, LLC

275 Market Street, Suite 469

Minneapolis, MN 55405

612-341-4020

golive@gigioliveinteriors.com

www.gigioliveinteriors.com

LEFT This Lake of the Isles converted house to condo, combines timeless design elements, making it perfect for reading a book, watching a winter fire or sharing conversation with a friend.

ABOVE RIGHT The architectural detail in this early 1900s house is complemented by the drama of the magenta velvet dining chairs, for a formal or casual event.

When it comes to the high-end residential projects, Gigi Olive excels in design talent whether in project management, new construction, remodeling or redesign. Setting her apart from many others in her field, Gigi often uses feng shui—the ancient Chinese "art of placement" to achieve harmony with the environment—to enhance health, wealth, and happiness in interior spaces. Known for her conscientiousness, Gigi is also environmentally friendly while working on projects, preserving as many natural resources as she can in her designs by recycling and reusing materials wherever possible.

Whether Gigi is working with traditional or contemporary interiors, she always has her clients' best interests in mind. "A successful project is more than an exquisite design," she explains. "It involves building relationships that last for years and through multiple dwellings." She believes that working as a team and genuinely listening to her client's needs and desires, creates innovative solutions capturing each client's well-deserved dream.

During the two decades she has been creating beautiful and distinctive homes, Gigi has earned significant accreditations, including the ASID First Place Model Home Award in 2000 for her model home in Eden Prairie's Bearpath community. She also participated in the ASID Showcase Home Tour, featuring rooms in showcase homes in Minneapolis' Lake of Isles community and Minnetonka. In addition to being featured in several local and national publications, Gigi has served on the Board of the ASID Minnesota Chapter as well as on several design committees, classifying her as a true professional with unmatched skills. ■

Angela Parker
Allied Member ASID
Interior Places & Spaces

INTERIOR PLACES & SPACES

2940 Hampshire Avenue South

St. Louis Park, MN 55426

952-451-1960

alparker_ips@yahoo.com

www.alparker-ips.com

LEFT Monochromatic colors define this glamorous master suite reflecting romantic rosewoods and aged brick walls. Espresso leathers, ebony and rosewood furnishings contrast with a paper white vaulted ceiling to create an atmosphere of loftiness and repose.

ABOVE Modern barrel vaulted ceiling opposite Canadian red birch flooring, mixed with maple, cherry, and stainless steel create drama in the great room/media center. Complementing rich caramel walls are offset with furnishings in bold geometrics, black leather and soft suede.

ABOVE RIGHT Whimsical pendant lighting set the mood and accentuates the river like qualities of the Persian Brown stone. Two counter heights with graceful undulating curves designed for comfort and accessibility define the work zone.

Just when Angela Parker thought art in the form of drawing, painting, and pottery was her occupational calling, she heard architecture and design calling even louder. "I realized that architecture and design had my heart," she says. "I could use my drawing skills to create three-dimensional spaces and bring life to interiors." She now brings that life to Minneapolis environments as the sole proprietor of her firm, Interior Places and Spaces, energizing kitchens, great rooms, and master rooms through renovation.

To ensure this energy reflects the innermost character of her clients, Angela first interviews them, photographs their homes, takes various measurements, and selects the architect and/or contractor. She then draws interior spaces to determine the exterior sizes, selects exterior materials such as windows, stone, and roofing. After drawings that specify cabinets and built-ins are completed, she works with her clients to select materials and finishes such as carpeting, hardwood flooring, countertops, and lighting. "My client and I are a design team from the initial sketches to installing the artwork," she explains. "It truly is a wonderful experience for both the client and me."

Angela's clean, proportional style of design—she particularly enjoys modern design influenced by the characteristics of the Bauhaus or the colors of Africa—is accented with architectural detailing and contrasting finishes and texture. "My philosophy is to help my clients find the soul and spirit of their home," she conveys. "A home is a place where we can find blessing, comfort, peace, and joy, and to share those pleasures with all who enter our places and spaces." ■

Wendy Rostal, ASID
Rostal Design

ROSTAL DESIGN

6212 Maloney Avenue

Hopkins, MN 55343

952-938-9434

www.rostaldesign.com

LEFT Inspiration for color came from the warm tones of the stone flooring of this eclectic global mix dining room re-model. The bold draperies replace heavy shutters to frame the view of the patio and gardens out back.

ABOVE A welcoming entry is important. The woodwork has been lightened up and walls warmed up with paint, the chest of drawers and antique photos create a point of interest, balanced out with a place to sit. The pineapple lamp provides a welcoming glow at night.

ABOVE RIGHT This complete kitchen remodel uses a mix of light and dark finishes with a splash of color added for interest. Once a u-shaped kitchen, the new layout lends itself to multiple cooks and works great for entertaining.

Wendy Rostal discovered her passion for interior design when, while scanning the list of courses at the University of Minnesota, she landed on "Introduction to Interior Design," and her life was never the same. Her design professor was exceptionally enthusiastic about decorative arts; inspiring her decision to work as a designer. Today she holds a bachelor's degree in interior design with a specialization in art history—and owns her own firm.

Rostal began her Hopkins, Minnesota-based business in 1999. Since that time, she was elected to a board of directors seat for the American Society of Interior Designers, Minnesota Chapter. Her rooms in two showcase houses exemplified her work and earned her an ASID award. Her personal style, as profiled in magazines, tends toward the traditional—an elegant mix of antiques and bold colors that create warm, friendly rooms. Rostal's design process starts with listening. She sits with clients to prioritize their needs and develop the project scope. A project can come to fruition quickly or over the course of a year. In either case, a space with which her clients fall in love takes shape. "The plan is the generator, the plan is what determines everything; it is the decisive moment," she says, quoting modernist architect Le Corbusier. Rostal's inspirations often come from the things around her, ideas found in magazines or books, or from the natural environment.

If she has a favorite project, it is the one in which her client gets excited about every aspect and detail of the project and process. It is the project when the clients are willing to wait six months for that special piece of furniture or artwork because it will make the room perfect. When clients are truly interested in what is happening and truly understand the process, then the decisive moment is theirs. ▪

Krista Schwartz, Allied Member ASID

Indicia Interior Design & Furnishings

INDICIA INTERIOR DESIGN
& FURNISHINGS

1664 Hartford Avenue
St. Paul, MN 55116
651-204-6481
krista@indiciallc.com

LEFT Redesigned within the existing space, this rec room's attractive but practical design is ideal for a family with busy teenagers. Cherry cabinetry wraps two walls creating great storage for games and DVDs along with a daybed for relaxing. Two TV locations won't let you miss the game. Convenient snacking and clean-up with microwave, beverage cooler, sink and dishwasher at bar.

ABOVE RIGHT This master bedroom is located within the completely remodeled second floor of a home originally built in the 1950s. Details such as the arch opening and built-in window seat give the room charm associated with older construction. The furnishings are a blend of antique and new. And the soothing palette of blue and tan create a restful space to end your day.

It only took a few courses in communications and dramatic arts for Krista Schwartz to realize that another path beckoned her name: the path of interior design. And her firm, Indicia Interior Design & Furnishings, proves she went with the right one. Krista founded Indicia in 2002 as a full-service design firm, focusing on remodeling homes for the majority of her clients.

Krista creates interiors that are comfortable to live in, and that can easily evolve with time. Many of her designs begin with adding architectural details and cabinetry to enhance the characteristics of each client's home. "A great backdrop always makes for a pleasing room and a mix of materials and finishes add to the draw of these spaces. "I consider pattern and texture when selecting items because we are all tactile by nature." To determine the right mix, Krista involves her clients throughout the entire design process so she can really comprehend their personalities, interests, and needs. She believes that good listening is one of the greatest skills a designer can possess, because clients are always providing clues regarding how they live, and how their homes facilitate their lifestyles.

When pulling a room together, Krista never overlooks the value of the smallest design facets and details that provide elements of character: multiple fabrics, trims, embellishments, and exceptional accessories. Krista also loves working with color. "With six months of winter in Minnesota, I feel that we all need color within our spaces to feel cozy, content, and alive." ■

Julie Stark
Allied Member ASID

J. Stark Interior Design

J. STARK INTERIOR DESIGN

8831 Inverness Road

Woodbury, MN 55125

651-730-6289

jstarkinteriors@hotmail.com

LEFT The master bedroom with it's custom designed bedding, drapery, and rug. There is a small sitting area to the right of the bed, with a mirrored coffee-table. The millwork is painted in a pearlized paint and the ceiling is papered in a metallic burl design.

ABOVE We have been collecting round and oval mirrors of all different sizes and varying degrees of decoration in order to reflect the landscape in a very exciting and creative way. We started in the center and just kept adding on until there was no more room. it really is an exciting surprise when you turn the corner and see it!

ABOVE RIGHT The master bathroom. The draperies are custom designed and the cornice fabric is made of cellophane. The wallcovering is designer's guild paper. We added Swarovsky crystals for added sparkle.

An independent residential interior designer specializing in new home construction, Julie Stark is a creative thinker. She starts the design process by talking to her clients about their lifestyles, and then she makes it her mission to surpass their expectations. As a result, she once turned a client's master suite into a portrayal of "reflection" by choosing mirrored nightstands and a mirrored coffee table, reflecting fabrics (she even had the drapery panels laminated to add sheen), ceiling papered in a metallic burl, pearlized-painted millwork, and a silk and wool rug for shine and texture. To add a truly unique touch, she hired an artist to create a mirrored mosaic on the backsplashes of the cabinets, found a mirror collage to capture the outdoor light in the sitting room, chose an upholstered cornice fabric actually made with cellophane, and added Swarovski crystals to the designer's guild wallcovering for extra sparkle. "The project resulted in a room that was exceedingly peaceful, inspiring, reflective, and personal," she recalls.

During her 27 years of concept-driven work, Julie has earned many prestigious awards. She has also completed numerous homes for the Parade of Homes. Additionally, she is an ASID allied member with a BS degree in interior design and a minor in studio arts from the University of Minnesota. While she certainly has the credentials, what is the real secret to her success? "I spend a lot of time and energy discussing the desired look and feel of the home and/or room with my clients," she says. "And then I turn it into the type of design that makes people 'feel' something."

LEFT A warm, book-matched mahogany paneled ribbon, combined with cherry floors and Douglas fir timbers, wrap this front entry, formal dining room and library in this Mississipi River home.

RIGHT An Indonesian teak and copper fireplace mantel help background Mark's designed oversized ottoman and cocktail table concept that connects all seating for intimate conversation.

Mark Suess, Allied Member ASID

Mark Suess Designs

Interior designer Mark Suess was designing his own traditional European style home with hand-crafted Indonesian furniture when he realized that he was limiting himself. Thinking "outside the box," he figured that Indonesian artists who could hand craft such beautiful tables, armoires, and cabinets could exquisitely hand craft the pieces for his home as well. So he ventured to the island nation, sketched out the desired woodworks, doors, and furniture for the traditional artisans, and shipped the finished pieces of his new home back to America.

Just like Mark defied formality with unconventional design for his own house, he often brings new and unique ideas to his clients' projects. "I love to travel and reflect different cultures and concepts in my work," he comments. A natural observer, he is constantly taking note of his environment to find ideas that he can merge with materials to create beautiful and useful interiors. These "borrowed" ideas in combination with his personal imagination have led to several revered projects, including the pool house he designed on the shores of Lake Superior in Duluth. The pool house was a new addition to a historical 10,000-square-foot Tudor Revival style home built in 1914 by John Killorin, who made his fortune in lumbering, mining, and wholesale hardware. The owners were particularly concerned with preserving the surrounding landscape. Mark alleviated this concern by designing the pool house as an Indonesian teak-carved English conservatory surrounded by garden follies reminiscent of the Victorian world

travelers who incorporated exotic architectural concepts and treasures into garden folly structures. The follies were well positioned as focal points to lead the eye to the property's striking views of Lake Superior. Mark was again inspired to assimilate the Indonesian culture into his designs when he completely transformed a colonial white home into a teak-carved timber-framed Mississippi River mansion and designed a teak-carved library and kitchen cabinetry for a Scottsdale, Arizona, home overlooking Pinnacle Peak Mountain.

To start the design process, Mark likes to meet with his clients at the project site. After listening to their ideas and desires, he suggests design concepts that he feels will work for them and encourages discussion, carefully noting their feedback. "I listen to what they have to say and deliver what they are really asking for," he says. Mark then pulls samples together to complete the design in his mind—he usually knows how he plans to design a space during the first meeting with a client—and qualifies each selection with availability and "build-ability." He also sketches the settings via floor plans

ABOVE LEFT A 300-year old Aubussun rug, foots Mark's bed design consisting of four Lotus flower bed posts.

LEFT Mark's design for the chair-side table was inspired by a brass serving tray he spotted in an Indonesian cafe.

ABOVE Mark purchased the master bedroom door knockers at a flea market in Rome, Italy. The carvings were designed to complement.

RIGHT Reclaimed Canadian warehouse timbers top off the commercial function of the food element carvings of this gourmet kitchen.

and 3-D renderings, which include colored illustrations of architectural details and furnishings, in various ways himself. This rendering then becomes the instruction sheet for executing the project.

Mark commenced his career in interior design after completing architectural technical school training and working as a draftsman for a retail/design architectural firm. While attending college, he started working in a high-end department store in the home furnishings department, where he became acquainted with the buying and merchandising process. Finding the furniture lines easy to sell, he pursued the interior design profession as a designer as well as a retailer. Mark regularly searches the globe to find one-of-a-kind pieces that make a statement and then often uses them in his own designs.

With 28 years in the profession, Mark is an ASID member at the state and national levels and is certified by the Minnesota Board of Architecture, Engineering, Land Surveying, Landscape Architecture, Geoscience, and Interior Design. To refine his skills, he attended and graduated from Mike Lin's Graphic Workshop—a workshop designed by registered landscape architect, ASLA member, and ASAI member Mike Lin for people seeking to improve their graphic skills and proper attitude in drawing—and a workshop in Rome Italy, taught by Purdue University's Professor of Landscape Architecture Greg Pierceall. All in all, Mark's background and certifications have showed him how to design in any style for projects ranging from residences and funeral homes, to high-tech corporations and healthcare offices.

ABOVE LEFT This 15-seat home movie and live-performance theatre is built underground, below the homes front circular driveway.

TOP Themed, carved Indonesian doors grace the entry of this home theatre lobby.

ABOVE A staged ticket booth, candy counter and popcorn maker add authenticity to the "Game Room" lobby.

Regardless of the project's size and scale, Mark's motto is, "I start from where people will be. Then I consider what they will do and from there I surround them with function and style." By thinking creatively and embracing new solutions, maintaining open lines of communication with his clients, and offering them options that he knows they will like, Mark has been able to design spaces with originality and worldliness without sacrificing comfort and practicality. ◼

MARK SUESS DESIGNS

1209 West Saint Germain Street

Saint Cloud, MN 56301

320-259-1868

mark@marksuess.com

RIGHT Gas-flamed light fixtures, salvaged Indian doors and reclaimed Indonesian teak flooring set the mood for this wine-tasting room.

BELOW Wine cellar air conditioner is disguised by small kitchen pass-thru shutters reclaimed from "Uzbekistan".

Lola Watson, Allied Member ASID
Lola Watson Interior Design, LLC

LOLA WATSON INTERIOR DESIGN, LLC

275 Market Street, Suite 564

Minneapolis, MN 55405

(612) 604-1661, (612) 604-1662 fax

www.lolawatson.com

LEFT Careful marriage of Federal period antiques with comfortable "come sit in me" furniture creates happy lakeside living for this young family of five.

ABOVE By painting and glazing existing cabinetry, the budget allowed for a custom designed island fitting the needs of a downsizing couple in this Edina Townhome.

ABOVE RIGHT Changing the traffic flow to direct active children in this remodeled Wayzata home offers a richly textured and inviting space for the adults of the family.

Designer Lola Watson brings a unique perspective to her work. Along with her training and 30-year background in interior design, Lola was a professional opera singer who still performs on occasion. Her career in opera took her around the world, exposing her to many different cultures and lifestyles. She brings that expanded sense of aesthetics to her clients. "I realized that the world was full of options and it would be a shame not to use those many choices to benefit my clients."

For Lola, her work—and her reward—is all about creating aesthetically pleasing homes that are as functional as they are beautiful. "It's there that I hope my clients can refresh and restore their spirits." It's important to her that she encourages her clients to raise their own aesthetic awareness. "Even the most mundane item or task can have an inherent beauty, if it's well and thoughtfully designed," Lola says. "Just because something is functional doesn't mean its form can't be beautiful."

It is that challenge to merge functional and pleasing environments with her clients' unique personalities that especially appeals to Lola. "If I can help my clients pay attention to the details of their lives, we'll be able to create environments that will help them live fully and comfortably." Lola says. "It's a lot like singing opera: Every night you have a new audience, and no matter how many times you've given the performance, this audience deserves your very best." ■

Deborah Beal
Wegener, ASID

Deborah Beal Wegener Interiors, Inc.

LEFT Whether enjoying afternoon tea or entertaining friends for cocktails, this room is a comfortable welcoming retreat. Like all good design, the room reflects the homeowner's personal tastes, beautifully showcasing beloved collections of Herend bunnies and Staffordshire dogs, as well as fine, rare books.

ABOVE RIGHT An exquisite 19th century mirror sets the tone for this formal dining room. Flowing silk draperies, a hand-cut crystal chandelier, and stately furnishings give the room a sense of grandeur without stuffiness.

Family is important to Deborah Beal Wegener, and her designs reflect it. It was the love of the family's grandfather that drove a lakeside retreat project, where all of the children and grandchildren helped collaborate on the plan. Fulfilling the wishes of young and old alike, Deborah installed an indoor pool, and a soda shop—all the things the large, extended family could ever dream about. In the end, the design was so perfect, one of the family members sought out Deborah for her next project—a 28-stable working horse farm in Minnesota with a distinctly Kentucky feel.

It is a typical result for the Minnesota-based interior designer, who spends a lot of time at the beginning of a project just getting to know her clients. Deborah tries to understand how they live, what makes them happy or unhappy; and her efforts are so successful, her clients' children often hire Deborah for their homes when they get older. "It makes me so happy," she says, "because it tells me they enjoyed the home we designed for them when they were growing up, and that they want in their own way to replicate the feeling that we gave to their home. It's more about the home than the house."

For Deborah, home has been Minnesota. After graduating with honors from the University of Iowa, she went to work in the design department at Jordan Marsh in Boston, and eventually moved back to the Midwest to start her own firm, Deborah

ABOVE Retro elements with a modern touch make this bathroom a comfortable guest retreat. Board-and-batten wainscoting, black and white octagonal floor tiles, and carefully selected accessories complete the look.

ABOVE A wonderful Federal bull's eye mirror flanked by hurricanes dress the room's fireplace. Antiques from C.W. Smith in Minneapolis make this the perfect spot to relax by the fire on chilly nights.

Beal Wegener Interiors Inc. Working in Boston was a valuable experience, she says, for it gave her a sense of what makes this country's architecture distinctly American—and a fine understanding of American antiques.

Today, she tries to honor the architecture of a building, and create an architectural focus if a building doesn't have one. "My main philosophy is that a room cannot have two stars," she says. "You have to decide whether that's a paint color, a beautiful oak floor, wonderful Palladian windows—just the same as you can't wear rings on every finger. You have to think of layering-in the background. The design loses its punch if there are too many items."

To create the desired effect, Deborah works closely with a wide selection of contractors, artisans, architects and tradespeople—all the while controlling the project's total direction. "My firm is about designing the entire project, incorporating treasured family pieces, helping clients select new things, and bringing it all together."

Yet Deborah has undertaken such wide-ranging projects as a firm on Wall Street, a medical clinic in St. Paul, and a Low Country cottage in Savannah, Georgia. "I like to take jobs that pique my interest, large or small, if I can make an impact and help the clients interpret what they want. It's the way I've run my firm for 25 years."

In that time, the work that she started in Minnesota has spread across the country, with Wegener traveling from state to state to work on her clients' homes. They have become like an extended family; and when each project is done, it reflects her clients well. ◼

DEBORAH BEAL WEGENER INTERIORS, INC.

19550 Muirfield Circle

Shorewood, MN 55331

952-470-0948 F: 952-470-1157

dbwinteriors@mindspring.com

BELOW The contemporary living room is a study of natural, textural elements. Great, white pine timbers accented with exposed steel beams support an airy loft space. A grand, 20-foot stone fireplace sets the tone for this architecturally unique home.

Sarah Wood
Allied Member ASID

Sarah Wood Interiors

SARAH WOOD INTERIORS

1775 Buerkle Road

White Bear Lake, MN 55110

612-414-6758

swinteriors@yahoo.com

LEFT Casual refinement found in sophisticated southwest furnishings enhance this living room, making it feel cozy yet at the same time grand. Warmth of color palette and soft furnishings contribute to an inviting ambiance.

ABOVE From paintings to sculpture, local artists works provide a visual focal point in this home. Textural fabrics and custom made furnishings provide the sophisticated backdrop for the owner's collections.

ABOVE RIGHT This indoor pool bathroom reflects the homeowners eclectic taste of neoclassical design blended with modern styling. The cabinetry's chemetal laminate shows in a beautiful, even illumination with colors of a sunset. Etched glass with inset metal stylizes the neoclassical, harmonizing with the more modern black granite and checkered tiled walls.

When asked how long she has been an interior designer, Sarah Wood replied, "In my heart, since childhood." While she did, at one time, rearrange her family's furniture and accessorize with her father's antique collections, these days, she is official with a degree in interior design from the University of Minnesota, 14 years of professionally practicing residential interiors under her belt, and her own design firm in White Bear Lake. Internally, she keeps her firm small and considers the tradespeople she teams with her extended office. Outside of this office, Sarah prefers to initially meet with her clients in their home so they can openly discuss their psychological needs, dreams, and visions involving design, and then prioritize those needs based on the perceived budget.

The back of Sarah's business card reads, "Home is, after all, where the heart is, and the memories, and the moments of the profoundest well being." Expounding on the quote, Sarah says, "I believe that a home should enliven the spirit, not diminish it. It should be a nurturing place to relax, reinvent, and feel genuine happiness." With this belief, Sarah tells her clients to splurge when necessary and that the first step to lasting contentment in a well-designed home involves focusing on what is really important to them as homeowners. From that, she designs with attention to detail and in line with her clients' own stylistic sensibilities. "I am providing a benefit to others," Sarah says. "To me, that is a meaningful life." ■

Photographers Credits

Index of Design Firms

Michele Eich, *Eich Interior Design*. See page 45.